Before Lynn

Before Lynn

Sheila Cordwell

ATHENA PRESS
LONDON

BEFORE LYNN
Copyright © Sheila Cordwell 2010

All Rights Reserved

ISBN 978 1 84748 730 8

First published 2010 by
ATHENA PRESS
Queen's House, 2 Holly Road
Twickenham TW1 4EG
United Kingdom

Printed for Athena Press

This book is dedicated to Brian and Kevin, my wonderful sons, in the hope that you will both understand me better. Love, Mum

Wartime in Greenford

Mum and I huddled together, under the stairs, in the darkness of the cupboard, listening and waiting. The doodlebug had stopped, and there was a long silence. We waited for the dreaded explosion, Mum holding me tighter. Would it be near us? Would we be killed?

The all-clear siren wailed, and we emerged from the darkness of the cupboard, saved again.

We often had to do this, as we didn't always have time to get to a shelter for safety.

The Anderson shelter in our back garden was full of water and frogs so it was never used.

We either went up the road to Mrs Osbourne's shelter, or across the road to Mrs Hunt's.

Mum and I would get under their large kitchen table, with Emily and Bill Hunt and their children, David and Margaret. I think their other son, Gordon, was in the army. Mum got on well with Emily, and after the war we had some lovely parties at their house.

Mrs Osbourne and her family were all rather large people and their garden shelter got very crowded. Sometimes the air raid would last all night and we would try to sleep down there.

When we emerged in the morning, we would look to see if our homes had been damaged.

Mrs Osbourne would keep a chamber pot just outside the doorway to the shelter, and she would go outside and use it even in a raid. I can still picture her large backside squeezing through the doorway!

Suffolk

I was born on 10 December 1937.

My mum was taking a bus ride to Oulton Broad to see her friend, Kath, when I decided to make my appearance!

It was a breech birth, which meant I came into this world feet first, and I've had trouble with them ever since!

We lived close to the sea at Pakefield in Suffolk.

My mother, Phyllis Howlett, was born at Humbleyard near Bungay, into a very poor family. Her father was a cowman and every Michaelmas, they had to move on, as they lived in tied cottages. She told me that they used to put the cat in a sack, so that it couldn't see where it was going!

My grandfather, John, resembled King George V. I only saw him once, when he was very ill, and he was lying on a black horsehair settee. He took my hand and placed a crown coin into it.

I went to see Nana Howlett when she lived in Bungay. We must have gone by coach, as Dad didn't have a car back then. She was a big woman with large legs that were covered with wrinkly stockings. She always wore a hairnet and a crossover floral pinafore (resembling Nora Batty!). Mum used to say that she had dropsy, but I never knew what that was.

I loved going to stay at her house, and the smell of pinks still reminds me of walking down her long garden path. On either side grew cottage garden flowers, Canterbury bells, delphiniums, poppies and Michaelmas daisies. The shingle path led round the house to a well at the back. This was never used, as it had frogs in it! They either got their water from next door's well, or from the pump across the road. There was a rainwater butt by the back door, used for washing.

When Granddad died, Nana took in a lodger to help around the house and garden; his name was Albert. He would catch rabbits and shoot pheasants and they would hang on the shed in the back garden.

Another of his jobs was to empty the bucket in the 'lavvy'. This was a small wooden shed which housed a fixed toilet seat with a bucket underneath and a trap door at the back. Hanging from a string were squares of newspaper. I hated going in there because of the smell and the flies! Albert would remove the contents daily, and dig them into the ground. He grew a lot of vegetables, fruit and lovely strawberries. If he couldn't find a nice one for me, he would put his hand through next door's fence and take one of theirs.

Nana's front room had faded willow pattern wallpaper that was covered with lots of photographs. The front door led into this room. Beside it was a small window that had geraniums on the windowsill blocking out the rest of the light. On either side were two large pictures of soldiers in First World War uniforms. One sitting and one standing, and they both had dogs at their feet.

In front of the fire was a circular table covered with a cloth, on top of which was an oil lamp surrounded by more framed photographs. Beside it was a large Windsor chair and a rocking chair, and in the corner of the room was the black horsehair settee, which was most uncomfortable.

The mantelpiece above the black fireplace was covered with a velvety fringed cloth, and on top of this were a pair of Stafford-shire dogs and a clock. There were also some brass objects that I used to play with, when I wasn't making up tunes to her hymn book.

There was always a fire in the grate and a kettle warming on a shelf beside a saucepan of potatoes, which had been there all morning! On the uneven tiled floor was a large piece mat. These used to be very popular, and were made by pulling odd pieces of material through a length of sacking with a hook. This room led into a small kitchen which had a large stone sink and an oven in the wall where the bread was baked. From the low ceiling hung a birdcage with one canary in it; there used to be two, but one died on the same day as Granddad.

This kitchen housed a huge walk-in larder. Inside was a large marble shelf to keep things cool. People didn't have a fridge in those days.

On this shelf would be butter, bacon and meat and a large

bowl of strawberries. Underneath, on the tiled floor would be a bucket of milk (which always tasted off, and put me off tea!). I can still remember the smell of this room.

Opposite the larder door was another that opened towards you when you pulled the latch down.

Very steep stairs rose up to Nana's bedroom on the left, and an open area on the right that had a bed behind a curtain.

I suppose this is where Albert would have slept, but when my parents came to stay, he slept on the settee downstairs.

I used to sleep beside Nana, who always smelt of wintergreen. She had a big black metal bed that had brass knobs on each corner. The bed was covered with a patchwork quilt. This room had a very small fireplace, and on the mantleshelf above it was a vase with some birds' feathers in it, and there were also various seashells as well. Her bed was very high and very comfortable. I would be put to bed with a colouring book and pencils, and eventually would fall asleep while everyone would walk down the road for a drink in the Duke of York pub.

Some days we would take a long walk down to the market-place in Bungay to do some shopping, and sometimes we walked in the opposite direction and across the heath. This was a very large area covered in heather and gorse bushes. But I would be delighted if I found some harebells. They were so pretty and delicate and I would pick a few to take back and draw.

Sadly, these things that I remember about Bungay are no longer there. My parents returned many years later and the house and garden had been modernised.

My Parents

My mum, Phyllis, had two older sisters, Maud (Maudie) and Edith (Edie). There was also brother Lenny (Sonny) who used to tease them. She told me that he used to open the trap door at the back of the 'lavvy' and tickle their bums with a stick!

All Mum's clothes were hand-me-downs, and her feet used to hurt so much in her small shoes that she used to cut the tops off and cool her feet under the village pump!

One of her jobs was to clean out the grate and make up and light the fire before she went to school, which was miles away.

Sometimes, when her dad was working in the fields, she would take him his dinner. One day, as she was getting over a stile with a can of stew, she fell and spilled the contents on the ground. She scooped it all up, earth as well, and put it all back in the can. She never said anything, and he ate it all up and never knew.

Another story she told me was when her teacher asked the class to bring some material to school to make peg bags. As she didn't have any, she cut a square out of the back of a gingham dress that she didn't like. She took it to school and made a lovely peg beg. She nearly got away with it, but one day a photographer was coming to take a school photograph, and they were told to wear their best dresses. Mum ran home and unpicked the peg bag, and sewed it back into her dress!

I don't know very much about my dad's early life. His name was Gordon and he was the illegitimate son of Clara Read. I was told that his father might have been an Italian sailor who got lost at sea. She brought him up on her own in very poor circumstances, in what looked like a small barn with a ladder outside leading to the top floor!

To make a living, Clara took in sewing. Times must have been very hard until she met and married Mr Boor.

They then had two sons, Marcus and Jack, and a daughter named Simone, and they then moved from Beccles Road to Kirkley.

When Gordon was old enough, he worked for Mr Tuck in Beccles and he drove a Bedford truck, delivering potatoes, mostly to fish and chip shops.

My mum's jobs ranged from being a chambermaid at Somerleyton Hall to being shop assistant and a waitress. Once when she was serving some Americans, they asked her if they had any latrines. Thinking that it might be something to eat, she said, 'I don't think we have any today.' It was when she worked at a fish shop that she met my dad. She had fair hair and pale blue eyes, and Dad had black hair and a dark complexion.

They got married in Ditchingham Parish Church, on 20 April 1935 – and it snowed!

They then moved to Pakefield Street, opposite the Trowel and Hammer pub; Mum said that once I crawled across the road, and they found me in the pub. I can still remember that uneven tiled floor. So this is my background.

Greenford

When I started to crawl, it was obvious that I had trouble breathing, and I was diagnosed as having asthma. World War II threatened, and my parents thought that the East Coast was vulnerable. So we went to stay with mum's sister Maud who lived in Hanwell, Middlesex. Uncle Jack was away in the army, and they had three children at that time. We stayed with them until accommodation could be found. The first place got bombed before we moved in! There couldn't have been much choice, as we ended up living in the top half of a terraced house in Greenford. My parents paid rent for two bedrooms and a box room, which got converted into a kitchen.

Mum was a very good cook, and on limited rations, produced some lovely meals in this tiny kitchen. There was a small gas oven, an old drop-leaf table and chairs, with a dresser for plates, dishes and cups and saucers, and bread, biscuits and tinned food. She used a copper on top of the cooker to boil the washing and carry it across the landing to rinse it out in the bath.

When I was very young, Mum would wash me in front of the fire in a large tin bath. This was kept downstairs, on the coal house door. One night, after I had been bathed and had my nice clean nightie on, I stepped back and fell into the water! Mum was not pleased.

There was only one upstairs toilet and bath, which we had to share with the downstairs tenants. When I was older, to save water, I would be first to have a bath, then Mum and then Dad. We used the same water, which had to be no higher than six inches! The gas and electricity were both on a shilling meter, which meant you had to keep a good supply of coins, or else you were running to a neighbour. Many times we were left in the dark, and of course there was always the odd power cut, so you had to keep a good stock of candles.

We were given the top half of the back garden, which had the Anderson shelter and an apple tree.

As Dad wasn't in employment, he was recruited into the fire brigade, and although he was stationed at Greenford, he often had to help out with the firefighting at the London docks during the Blitz.

In the early days, I slept in the back bedroom with my parents, and the other room was made into a sitting room. It had a tiny fireplace that smoked, even though Dad made various hoods to set over it. Every spring, the chimney sweep came. This meant covering everything with old sheets because of the soot. Then afterwards there was a spring clean. The coal was delivered by lorry, in sacks that were emptied into the coal shed out the back (which meant walking through the house). It would then be brought upstairs and put into a coal box by the fire. This was called a box curb, and there was another one the other side of the fire that held the firewood. They had leather tops and you could sit on them and warm your legs. But you had to be careful, or you got red legs!

There was an oval drop-leaf table, with barley twist legs, two matching chairs and a sideboard. At Christmas there would be bottles on the top. Mum would give the insurance man and the rent man a drink of either sherry, advocaat or something called Green Goddess. There was also ginger wine. We had a brown Rexine settee and two armchairs. This, then, was 89 Windmill Lane, where we lived for about fifteen years.

Windmill Lane was very long and had a cemetery at one end and a covered market at the other. I loved going there with Mum. It had a large wet fish stall (Mac Fisheries), lots of fruit and veg, and even a meat counter. You could get dress and curtain material and all sorts of sewing aids. You also got clothes, underwear, stockings, socks and shoes, and of course flowers. Sometimes there would be a man outside selling fluffy chicks from a cardboard box; of course, I always wanted one. I did get a rabbit one time. Mum and I went by bus to Shepherd's Bush market and bought a lovely white one. We brought it home in a carrier bag, which it wet, and got out and hopped around the bus! Somehow we got it home, and Dad built a hutch for it in the back garden. However, this was short-lived, as it jumped out of my arms, broke his leg, and died.

Greenford had two cinemas, the Playhouse and the Granada (I think that's now a bingo hall). There was a lovely wool shop and a hairdresser's. I remember a butcher's, a Home and Colonial and a small Sainsbury's which had a black and white tiled floor, and the shop smelt of cheese and bacon. You would have to queue up for these at either of the long counters that ran down each side of the shop. Once you got your provisions using your ration book, you then paid a lady at the end of the store. We also had a 'Woolies' and Lovells, the sweet shop. Opposite, were Dorothy Perkins and the Fifty Shilling Tailors. Then further up was a Provident shop (where you got clothes and household linen on tick). There was a patisserie, which sold lovely cakes and break, and a tea shop at the back, where we went for a special treat. In contrast to this, was a busmen's café, where I had a Saturday job selling ice creams and lollies; this was later on.

If you went to the park, you would walk past, the clinic, the library and the police station.

We were a bus ride away from Wembley, and would often go to watch Wembley Lions play ice hockey, or the Harlem Globetrotters play basketball, which was very entertaining.

Outside the market was where the buses lined up. You could go to lots of places, including, Hanwell, Ealing and Ealing Broadway. When I was older, we sometimes went to Chiswick or the Shepherd's Bush Empire. We saw Max Wall, Max Miller, Sid Millward and his City Slickers, Winifred Atwell and many others. The other treat was to go to the 'pictures', though this was more for Dad, as we always saw John Wayne, Edward G Robinson or James Cagney movies. I remember them all!

I don't remember a lot about the war years, but I know I missed a lot of infant and junior schooling because of ill health. I was given a gas mask. It had pink ears, to look like Mickey Mouse, but I couldn't breathe with it on.

As I was such a delicate child, I easily got colds and then bronchitis. I was very underweight and had a poor appetite, so Mum would get me a small tin of blackcurrant purée, which was full of vitamin C, and from the clinic, concentrated orange juice and cod liver oil and malt, which I absolutely loved. To obtain these, Mum had to get my identity card stamped (I still have this).

My tonsils were removed when I was about five, and I had my appendix removed two years later. This was an emergency, and the only hospital available at that time was at Hemel Hempstead. This meant of course that I didn't see much of my parents.

I also remember being very poorly with double pneumonia. I was on M&B tablets, which made me think that the room was spinning!

I spent a lot of time lying on the settee, with blankets and pillows, listening to the radio. This became my 'education'.

I would listen to everything, from Housewives' Choice, Workers' Playtime, Listen with Mother, Woman's Hour, Children's Hour, Toytown (with Larry the Lamb) to Dick Barton, Special Agent. I loved music, popular and classical. I knew all the tunes and the names of composers.

I also loved serials, and couldn't wait to hear the next instalment of *Ballet Shoes* by Noel Streatfield. (This was to start my love of the ballet.)

In the evening we would sit by the fire and listen to *The Man in Black* and be scared by the voice of Valentine Dyall. On Saturday afternoons, I would listen with Dad to the football results and wait with anticipation to see if we had three draws.

Mum used to look after me all day at first, but later on she had to go out to work to pay for the doctor's bills. There was no NHS in those days.

She would bank up the fire with coal dust, then go off to the school, where she had a part-time job in the kitchen. Sometimes she would bring home a canister with some shepherd's pie in it, and sometimes, apple crumble.

Mrs Hunt, from across the road, would pop in to see if I was all right and to check on the fire.

I loved to draw and copy the advertisements that were on the front of the *Daily Mirror*. These were black and white illustrations of ladies fashions for C&A.

It must have been a difficult time for Mum, looking after me. Sometimes the asthma attacks were very bad and prolonged. I would lie for hours in a pool of sweat, trying to breathe. When I went to infant school, I was on ephedrine tablets. These made you sleepy, and one day I fell asleep at my desk, and when I woke up, everyone had gone home except for the teacher. Another time, Mum took me by bus to have injections in my thigh. That was until the day I struck out at the doctor and the needle broke in my leg. 'That's it,' he said, 'she can't have any more.'

After that, I went to several hospitals in London. We would go by Underground to St Mary's in Paddington, to the Brompton Hospital and Great Ormond Street. At one of these, I had to go for breathing lessons. Unfortunately, the lifts were still out of order (because of the war), and by the time I had walked all the way up to the top, I was in a state of collapse. They had a job getting me to breathe, let alone do exercises!

I have lots of memories of London: waiting for trains at various stations, the escalators, and even tramlines on the road. Coming out of a station one day, I saw a huge billboard advertising the film *Spring in Park Lane*, with Anna Neagle and Michael Wilding pictured dancing across it.

We went to another place to try out inhalers. One was plugged into the wall and I was supposed to inhale from it. However, it made such a noise that I wouldn't go near it. So we were given one that Mum had to administer because it was too large for me to handle. Later on they brought out a smaller version which I was able to take to school and use myself. This had a small brown glass top which had two projections that had rubber stoppers in the end. A little anti-asthma inhalant would be poured in and then inhaled by squeezing the rubber bulb attached. This brought instant relief.

I didn't go out much in the winter and I didn't know what snow felt like. One day when Mum was out I managed to open a side window and get a handful of snow off of the windowsill. It looked and felt amazing to me.

We didn't have double glazing in those days and the winters were very harsh. The inside of the windows would get frosted up and I was fascinated by the beautiful patterns on the glass. It was hard to keep the rooms warm at night because the fireplaces were so small; even when they were banked up with coal dust, they would still go out. Coal was expensive and sometimes difficult to get. Occasionally we had to make do with some cheaper stuff that used to spit out across the room! Every spring, the chimney had to be swept. This meant every item in the room had to be covered with old sheets in readiness for the chimney sweep and all his brushes. Even so there would be quite a mess, and Dad would keep the soot for the garden – I'm not sure what for.

When all the mess was cleared up, it was time to decorate. The walls would be emulsioned. Mum chose apple green for the front room, which looked OK, but then she decided to make it look like wallpaper.

She put a piece of rag over three fingers, then dipped them in some maroon paint and dabbed this on top of the green. This was known as stippling, and was fashionable at the time. The trouble was, it looked neat to start with, but by the time she got to the last wall, the shapes got larger and rougher! Not content with this, she then used some gold paint and repeated the process!

Mum was very house-proud and would keep all the brown lino floors highly polished. One day, when I was older, I thought I would surprise her and washed them. She was not pleased.

I remember a picture in the bedroom. It had a black background and there was a full moon shining on a lady in a crinoline dress, standing on a bridge. I thought of this whenever I heard 'Moonlight becomes you', sung by Bing Crosby.

After the War

8 May 1944: Victory in Europe was being celebrated. I was seven years old, and Windmill Lane was getting ready for a huge street party. Everyone brought out their tables and chairs and placed them together all down the street. These were covered in sheets or tablecloths, then spread with plates of sandwiches, cakes, buns, biscuits, cold meats, sausage rolls, jellies and blancmanges and jugs of orange and lemonade. Music was being played and there were Union Jacks hanging from windows, and we each had one to wave. In my excitement to get out, I fell up our garden steps and cut my knee badly. I still bear the scars today, as well as another on the other knee, which I got on VJ day, when I did the same thing again!

In the evening, my friend Pat and I wandered around the other streets to watch people laughing and singing around huge bonfires, built in the middle of the road. It was wonderful!

Dad came out of the fire service and went to work at Pepsi-Cola. He would bring home bottles of it on his bike, and for a long time I would drink nothing else. Later on, the Corona man would come round and deliver us dandelion and burdock, cream soda and cherryade.

Another drink I really liked at that time was made from Creamola Foam Crystals. These were in a packet and you stirred a spoonful into a glass of water. You got this lovely lemony base with a thick creamy topping. Delicious!

Clothes and food were still rationed, and Mum made quite a lucrative business making slippers.

She would draw round people's feet onto cardboard, cut out the shape, then stitch coloured webbing around the edge in two layers and then two more pieces across the toes. This would be edged with braid and finished off with a pompom on top (all bought at the market, of course).

We also made our Christmas decorations. We stuck strips of

coloured paper together to make paper chains. We also made little figures from wool, which we put on our tiny Christmas tree. Mum taught me to knit, and we made kettle holders, tea cosies and scarves, then progressed to jumpers, gloves and socks.

One day, the word went round that they had bananas in the market, and everyone rushed up the road to join the queue!

I also remember the day that sweet rationing ended. Mum gave me some money and said I could go up the shops and buy whatever I liked. Of course I was spoilt for choice, but eventually I settled for a bag of sherbet lemons.

Halfway along Windmill Lane was the Holy Redeemer Church, where I used to go to Sunday school if I was well enough. It had a large hall, and when I was about ten, I went there twice a week to ballet lessons. I loved it, and I was trained by Miss Eileen Munford for about five months.

Then on 6 October, I went to the Royal Academy of Dancing at Holland Park, to take a Grade One exam. I remember my dress had got badly creased, and a kind ballerina there held it out over a radiator to get it smooth.

I managed to get a 'Commended' and very good marks for deportment. However, I had to give it up because of my health.

To make up for my disappointment, my parents managed to buy me a piano. When it arrived, the delivery men had to remove the banisters on the landing to get it into the front room! So then I started going to music lessons with Pat Hicks, who lived next door. We would catch a bus to Greenford Station, and walk to 2 Lincoln Close, where we were taught by Mrs Evans. She particularly liked Beethoven and she had a large bust of him, which would wobble when you played the piano. Pat lived with her parents, older brother and her grandparents. Her granddad made caravans in their back garden, and when they were finished and sold, the whole fence had to be removed to get them out. This usually drew a crowd. Luckily, they lived beside the alleyway that led up to the allotments.

My dad didn't have an allotment, as he grew all our vegetables in the back garden.

Our shelter was dismantled, and the concrete was broken up and made into a rockery. After digging the garden over with manure, Dad sowed seeds using a line as a guide. I can picture him now. His white singlet showed off his permanent tan – he loved the sunshine – and he always had a cigarette in his hand. He was a handsome man, and with his moustache he was not unlike David Niven.

Sometimes I would go to the allotment shop with him to buy seeds and things. I loved the different smells in there.

Pat got tired of going to music lessons, so I went on my own. I took my Preliminary Exam at the Guildhall School of Music Drama, where in 1950 I passed with Honours.

One Saturday when Mum was out shopping, I was practising my scales, when Guy, our downstairs neighbour, knocked on our door. He told me to stop making a noise as it annoyed him. This upset me so much that I never played the piano again.

Meanwhile, Pat was going old-time dancing with her parents, and winning medals. For each exam, she would have to have a new dress. My mum would make these. Each one a different colour and made with yards and yards of net!

On the other side of us lived Beryl, who was a lot older than me, but in the summer she would let me play in her tent. She had lots of little cups and saucers, pots and pans and also *Rupert Bear Annuals* to read.

Next door to Beryl was the Cliff family.

Mum didn't care for me going there as they were a bit 'rough', but I liked them. Margaret was about my age, and Michael was the youngest. I think there was another brother, Ronnie. Michael was always up to mischief. Once he scared the neighbours by hanging stark naked from the bedroom window, swinging backwards and forwards!

Another time, he threw a stone at the baker's horse. It bolted up the road, dragging the van of bread with the doors swinging about at the back. This was hotly pursued by a very irate delivery man!

In the school holidays I sometimes played with Margaret in her back garden. Among the overgrown grass and weeds was an old car chassis. It had battered bucket seats and Margaret and I would sit in these and pretend to go to the seaside. Later on, I was dissuaded from playing with Margaret as one day a man had exposed himself to her at the nearby park.

One day, the Cliffs got a goat and tethered it to a post in the middle of the garden. The object of this was to keep down the grass. Once clear, the post would be moved. However, one day the goat uprooted the post and made a dash for the allotments at the back of us.

This caused an uproar among the gardeners, as it started eating their vegetables and had to be chased off!

Mrs Cliff was a nice plump woman who, like me, also had asthma. She used to be a commercial artist and she showed me some artwork she had done; there were some poster colour adverts for toothpaste. The brushes in the glass tumbler were very realistic. She also had lots of books and she played a very old, out-of-tune piano.

There was another boy in our 'gang', but not for long. David Lapage was highly intelligent and had a huge stamp collection. He was very knowledgeable about different countries and other things. However, he couldn't ride a bicycle and we would all laugh at his attempts, especially when he fell into a hedge. He didn't really fit in. Then one day police cars arrived outside his house, and later on Mum told me that he had been found hanging, in a cupboard.

Further along the road lived the Watsons.

Maisie and Ernest couldn't have children of their own, so they adopted two, Michael and Carol. They were a very happy family and they were always doing things, like drawing, painting or stencilling. Maisie would stencil on the mirrors and put artificial ferns in vases on the walls. (On which were also flying ducks!) She would spend time playing cards, snakes and ladders, Ludo or dominoes with us. They too had an old piano.

Out the back, they kept chickens, and to feed them Maisie would boil up potato peelings. The smell was awful! One day, Ernest killed a chicken. He cut off its head and it ran around headless for ages. I don't know if they ever ate it.

Occasionally, Maisie would give herself a home perm. This would either be Pin-up or Twink. The only thing was, she would leave it on all day, and appear with a mass of frizz. She didn't seem to mind, though.

The Watsons were the first people in the street to rent a

television set, and on Sunday evenings we would go to watch *Sunday Night at the Palladium* with them. Maisie loved Tommy Cooper, and would go into uncontrollable fits of laughter.

Sometimes we would play cards, usually Queenie, or New-market as it's generally known. This would be for pennies, of course.

Maisie had a twin-tub washing machine. As well as clothes, she put in plastic curtains and even wellington boots! What a character she was.

Holidays

Sometimes we would go and stay at Auntie Maud's in Hanwell. This meant I would have to sleep at the foot of Yvonne's bed, and Brian, who was my age, would sleep at the foot of Joan's. Unfortunately Joan, who was the eldest, was mentally deficient and blind in one eye. It made no difference to us, but Auntie found her difficult to cope with. She would leave her in bed for hours, and she would rock to and fro so much that the bed would move across the floor! She was very strong and one day she put her hands around my neck and nearly strangled me! She didn't mean it, of course. Years later she went into a home where she was cared for until she died.

Cousin Brian was also a bit of a handful. He would climb out of the downstairs bathroom window and get up to all sorts of trouble around the estate. Eventually, he joined the army and took up boxing.

Yvonne was the youngest at that time; Auntie had another boy later on called Michael. Yvonne had lovely blonde ringlets. Each night these were made by winding rags around bunches of her hair. They stood out from her head and Brian would pull on them! I don't know how she managed to sleep on them.

Dad's sister, Simone, married Peter Graver and moved to King's Lynn. They had two daughters, Sylvia and Hazel. Later on, Billy was born. They lived with Nana Boor at 30 Bridge Street, next door but one to the Greenland Fisheries Museum. This was derelict at the time, and Sylvia said that there were ghosts in there. The back of Nana's house had been badly bombed, and we would play among the ruins. We often saw the odd rat running about, looking for maize from Paul's Mill.

The house had three floors, and in the attic were a rocking horse and a musical box. You turned a handle to wind it up, placed a metal disc on the top and, as it rotated, it got plucked and produced a beautiful tune. There were several of these discs. I loved it up there.

On Tuesdays we all walked down the cobbled high street to Tuesday market, which was much bigger than it is today. Mum and Auntie would buy fresh fruit and vegetables, as well as fish or a crab. On the way back, we would stop at Scuphams the butcher's, and buy meat and the best pork pies ever.

Some evenings, the grown-ups would go out for a drink. Sylvia, Hazel and I would be put into a double bed. We were told, if we were good, they would bring us back a chip bag each. Sylvia and I would tell each other ghost stories. Hazel would fall asleep before the cone-shaped bags of goodies arrived.

Nana Boor had long black hair with a centre parting and a fringe. The side pieces were plaited, then wound up and pinned over the ears. This style was known as 'earphones'. We loved to watch her undo them and brush out her waist-length hair before climbing up the narrow wooden stairs to bed. I remember she had a statuette of a lady holding up a bunch of cherries ready to eat. The cherries got broken off accidentally, so my dad replaced them with real ones. I wonder how long it was before she realised.

This old house had shopfront windows downstairs. One day, Sylvia and I were given some spare pastry, so we made some jam tarts. After they were cooked, we placed them in the window with a price ticket on. Imagine our surprise, when a man stopped and looked as if he might come in and buy one! However, he moved on. Auntie still had a Morrison shelter. It was used as a table, and underneath we children used to play or have a rest. I really loved my time at King's Lynn.

Apart from going to King's Lynn by train, we would get up early and catch a coach at the top of the road, and go to either Bungay, Lowestoft, Eastbourne or Hastings. Dad would carry a very heavy old leather suitcase tied up with a leather belt, and mum would carry a large holdall which had sandwiches and flasks of tea and cola. I found these journeys very long and boring.

When we went to Lowestoft, we would stay at my dad's brother's old house. Uncle Jack and Auntie Betty were very large. Their house was long and narrow with a privy out the back. Mum and I slept together in their double bed (which was reinforced with planks and very hard), and the bedroom floor sloped so much that we thought we would go out of the bedroom window feet first!

I liked Lowestoft. We would walk around the quayside and Dad would tell us about all the trawlers that used to come and unload their fish there. We would then go to the beach and I would amuse myself on the sand while Mum and Dad relaxed in deckchairs. After that we would have the best fish and chips ever, before going back to Auntie's. Uncle Jack was a coach driver, so he often didn't get back until late.

My memories of Eastbourne were of bad boarding houses, bad food and really bad weather! We spent most of the time walking round the shops or sitting in the bandstand to get out of the rain.

Hastings too was unreliable. I can still remember a very wet and windy visit to Fairlight Glen.

One day though, we walked along the promenade and came to the White Rock Pavilion. The notice boards outside advertised that Ted Heath and his band were playing that evening, so to make up for the awful time we were having, Dad went in and got us tickets. That evening we sat near the front and really enjoyed the music. Then Ted Heath introduced his singers. First there was Denis Lotis, then Lita Rosa came on, followed by a good-looking young man called Dickie Valentine, He had a wonderful voice and also did very good impressions of Johnnie Ray and Nat King Cole. I was in love! From that moment, I collected everything I could about him, and later on I bought his records.

As well as these holidays, we would go by bus to Kew Gardens or London Zoo for the day. I wasn't keen on all the walking, though, as I sometimes got an asthma attack. We also visited Madame Tussaud's and Windsor Castle. Another time we went blackberrying at Gerrards Cross. We missed the bus home and an American stopped and gave us a lift home in his very fast car.

From Greenford we could get to lots of nice places, one of them being Ruislip Lido. This was a vast expanse of water surrounded by sand and trees. It was just like being at the seaside. We would spend all day there, having brought food and drink with us. You could get deckchairs and buy ice creams, paddle or watch the boats. Then at the end of the day we'd catch the bus home, which stopped outside. Sometimes Maisie and the children would come along and join the fun.

Neighbours

One day when I came home from school, the flat had been transformed. My piano had gone from the front room, and in its place was a radiogram. Also there was a double divan, with a candlewick bedspread on it instead of the old gold silk one. This meant I now had the back bedroom to myself. This was soon adorned with pictures of Dickie Valentine.

We had several different neighbours living downstairs at 89 Windmill Lane. Mr and Mrs Rodgers were the first ones – an odd elderly couple. My dad used to keep his bike in the hall, and one morning he went downstairs, well wrapped up to go to work. Mr Rodgers appeared and asked him to enter their bedroom. He pointed to the ceiling saying, 'Look what you've done!' and held out some plaster. Dad looked up and Rodgers punched him in the face, knocking him to the floor. There was quite a commotion, and somehow Mum managed to get the police. (Nobody had a phone in those days.) I was told to stay in bed while the police were taking statements and Dad was having his bloodied face cleaned up. Later, there was a court case, and I could have been called upon to give evidence. What the Rodgers didn't know was that I was ill in bed and heard them banging on their ceiling to make the plaster fall down. What they hoped to gain from all this, I don't know, but I didn't have to go to court and Mr and Mrs Rodgers soon departed.

The next tenants were also unusual. We didn't see much of them; I know his name was Guy and he was always decorating. As we went down the stairs, we would try to see what he was doing, but usually the doors were closed. However, one day Mum and I caught a glimpse through their bedroom door. The walls were emulsioned pink, and in each corner he had painted an antelope leaping out of a circle, all done in gold. Another time they had left the living-room curtains open, so Mum and I had to take a peek. To our amazement, above the fireplace was the head of a knight in armour. It was made from plaster and also painted gold. We were stunned!

They didn't stay long, and then Joan and Ted Best came. They were a nice couple and they also brought along their cat called Cholmondeley (Chumly). Now we also had a cat, who was all black and called Tinker. He didn't take to this new neighbour, and it caused a lot of amusement watching them trying to pass each other on the stairs or in the hallway. They would squeeze against the walls on either side, spitting and swearing as they went!

At one time we had a budgerigar called Bluey. Thinking Tinker was out, Dad let it out of its cage. Suddenly, Tinker leaped up from behind the armchair, caught the bird, and that was the end of Bluey. Which was just as well, as I'd had allergy tests, and feathers and pollen gave me asthma. I was all right with Tinker, though his fur made my face itch a bit.

Art School

I was going to Coston Secondary Modern School for Girls. My asthma had improved, I had had my tonsils and my appendix out, and was enjoying a full day's education.

I excelled in history, English, needlework, science and music. I used to illustrate my textbooks and the plain covers on our school library books, so I was encouraged to sit for the local art school examination.

This meant submitting my work and going to Ealing School of Art for a day with several others.

We were taken to the top floor of this old building and we sat in a circle, and had to draw a bucket that was placed inside a chalk circle. It was a bit daunting, as there were life-size statues of naked men looking down at us! In the afternoon, we had to paint a picture. We then left, and got the 211 bus back to Greenford. Later I learned that I was the only one who passed the exam.

When I started in September, I was one of the first to go into the new building. This adjoined the old one, and sometimes we had lessons in that part. We had half a day's education, and the rest was for art work. We had a very stern headmaster, Mr Lightfoot, and we had to wear school uniform. In winter, the girls wore a navy gymslip with white shirt, navy cardigan and tie. In spring and summer, we wore a plain green dress with detachable collars and cuffs. I absolutely hated it, especially as it showed the slightest hint of perspiration, so I would wear my knitted cardigan even on the hottest day! The girls wore berets; the boys caps, and the badge had to face the front or you would be in trouble!

We also had navy blazers and raincoats. As I was short, my raincoat came down to my ankles. (My mum said I would grow into it, but I did feel silly in it.)

When we came out at the end of the day, the boys would remove their caps and the girls would take off their socks to try and look grown-up. But if Mr Lightfoot found out, you would have to stand outside his door!

I wasn't used to a mixed school, and was amazed at the boys' behaviour whenever a teacher left the room. I sat next to Brenda Clark, who was tall and shapely. She had long curly hair and a bust! She would carry her satchel under her arm, and walk with a swagger. In fact she was everything I was not, and she attracted looks from the boys.

I hadn't had any sex education; my mother presumed that I knew where babies came from. One Sunday, the *Mirror* published pictures of a birth and she wouldn't let me see it. I also didn't know about having a period, so I was alarmed when it happened. She told me not to worry and gave me a piece of towel and two safety pins, and told me to pin it to my vest! I learned that I was the last girl at school to get her 'monthlies', so I didn't feel so left out as a result.

One thing I clearly remember when I was there. A teacher came into class to tell us that King George VI had died that morning at Sandringham. We were very sad to hear the news, but this meant that his daughter, Elizabeth, would be crowned Queen.

London

I loved my two years at Ealing. I used to catch the 211 bus to Ealing Broadway, walking past a pet shop that had a toucan in the window. On one occasion, I saw Sid James looking in the window. This was not far from Ealing Studios.

At the end of term I had very good reports. As well as art work, we had to do general subjects. I particularly liked our form teacher talking about Greek mythology. But most of all I enjoyed dress design, plant drawing, craft work, lettering and pattern design; I wasn't so keen on Illustration. In the first year, we had to make smocks to cover our uniforms. These were of the same green material as our dresses and we had to do smocking round the cuffs and across the bust. We learned to weave scarves and make and embroider belts. I would have liked to have stayed at the school another three years and done life drawing, still life, oil and watercolour painting. Unfortunately my parents could not afford to keep me there.

I was unexpectedly summoned to the headmaster's office one day. He told me that he had recommended me to an agency in London. I was surprised, but also excited. I was the first student to leave before the end of term.

The advertising agency was in Covent Garden, close to the Royal Opera House. As it meant a change of trains, Mum came up with me the first time. We left the underground station and emerged into the hustle and bustle of the market. It was so colourful and exciting. We then walked towards the Strand and found the address. Koster and Murray was up several flights of stairs. In one room sat the two ladies who ran the business, and in another was a young lady who was drawing, and in a corner sat a little old lady, sewing. Her name was Miss Alberhari and the artist was Rita. This agency did a lot of work for *Woman* and *Woman's Own*. The illustrations in these magazines that showed you how to make things were also done here. Also, knitting patterns were designed, sent out to be made, then sent back here to be made up by Miss Alberhari, who was very sweet but didn't speak much English except for 'Oh, dear!' Mrs Koster had a beautiful daughter, Judy, who was a model, and Mrs Murray had a son called Michael who was a photographer. So Judy would model the garments, either for magazines or knitting patterns, and Michael would photograph them. Occasionally I would get a free jumper.

Sometimes, I was given money to get a taxi and deliver the artwork we had done to the magazines off Fleet Street, going past the Old Bailey. At Christmas time, we had to think up interesting things to do and make, such as melting down candles to make decorations. (Making a mess in a saucepan!) I was also one of the first people to learn how to use a knitting machine. I loved my time there.

Rita (who was the same age as Princess Margaret) and I became great friends, even though she was older than me. She had dark, curly hair and a pleasant face, upon which she applied thick, dark-toned pan-stick make-up, leaving her neck white! We had the same sense of humour and tastes in film stars. Sometimes I would be invited to spend the weekend at her home in Twickenham, and we would go to the cinema. We saw Gérard Philipe in *La Ronde*, Richard Burton in *The Robe*, and Laurence Harvey in *Romeo and Juliet*.

In my lunch break, I would walk down to the Strand, past the Lyceum, and go to the Army and Navy stores; or walk the other way, past Drury Lane Theatre and Covent Garden Opera House. One lunchtime I walked through the flower garden (under cover) and saw the barrow boys packing up. They started selling very early in the morning. I found myself in a street with a café, and went in and bought a cup of tea. Unfortunately for me, the cup was chipped and none too clean. This led to me getting gingivitis (inflammation of the gums), and it was extremely painful.

I had to stay at home; I couldn't eat or drink anything or even talk. During the day, I lay on Mum's divan in the front room. For some reason, Dad was at home, and as it was wintertime he made some tomato soup for himself. He pulled up a chair close to the fire with one hand, and the bowl of soup in the other, but it tipped and put out the fire!

I wanted to laugh but it hurt too much. Dad might have been at home recovering from a burst peptic ulcer. This happened one night and he was rushed into hospital, very ill.

I stayed at Koster and Murray's for about a year. I would get the tube home at night, standing most of the way with a basket full of fruit and flowers that the barrow boys had given me. Usually they were strawberries and carnations.

On one of these journeys, a good-looking young man and I got talking. We soon got used to looking for each other and he shared the carriage with me. Inevitably, I invited him home one evening. Mum and Dad discreetly went up the road to Maisie's when he arrived. However, I don't think he was impressed with our tiny flat, and after a goodnight kiss, I never saw him again – not even on the train.

One day, I spotted an advertisement for an office job at C&A. I still wanted to get into fashion design, and I thought that if I could get a foot in the door, I might get into their studio. The job was boring, mostly filing and simple line drawings of children's clothes. I tried to get further, but was told I was too young and needed experience. So after helping out downstairs on a sales day (which was horrendous!), I left.

My next job was just off Oxford Street and was upstairs in a block of flats in Maddox Street. This was a small business run by a little Jewish man called Mr Chalmers. He and another tailor cut out and made up garments in a sort of calico fabric. These were then modelled for clients by Joyce, his beautiful secretary.

I went to assist a young man who sat in a tiny room designing clothes. I would copy his work as fast as possible to be sent out to prospective buyers. Because there was no other room, a desk was set up for me in the showroom. This had several display cabinets that were full of jade objects. I had no idea about them until Mr Chalmers told me one day, that they were priceless items. In the flat above, lived Averil Angers a well-known radio comedienne at that time, and above her a lady who often carried a cello up and down the stairs.

I only stayed there for three months. I got tired of copying someone else's artwork and sitting alone in this showroom. Obviously this was before photocopiers were invented, which would have done the job quicker. The thing I missed most was going round the shops at lunchtime, especially Liberty's. Reluctantly I left Central London and the West End.

Perivale

It was about this time that Dad got a job at Hoovers on the Western Avenue, Perivale, Middlesex. Because of his experience in the fire service, he was now a security officer. Things were looking up for all of us, especially as there was a promise of a house to go with the job, when one came available.

Hoovers had a dance floor and stage and they held regular old-time dances there. Dad had seen young people about my age there when he was on duty, and he thought that I might be interested, as I was at a loose end. So I agreed to meet Dad one Thursday evening, and go upstairs to the dance floor and watch the dancers through the doorway.

There were no young people, and I was just about to go, when a very small, grey-haired man, came over and introduced himself to Dad and myself as Gerry. He told Dad he would take care of me, and led me to his table. I was introduced to his friends and then sat and observed. There were tables all round the hall, all occupied. The windows on both sides were draped with deep red velvet curtains, as was the stage. The MCs were Mr and Mrs Heath, and everyone danced to records.

Nervously, I let Gerry lead me onto the floor and show me how to do the various steps. He was an excellent teacher and dancer, and I was soon enjoying it, especially doing the tango. And so I agreed to get the bus every Thursday and join Gerry until I was confident enough to go to the Saturday night dance. This was always in full evening dress, which was a problem. However, Joan Best, who lived downstairs, gave Mum her old pale blue taffeta bridesmaid's dress. It was long, and had puff sleeves, and it had a belt with a buckle at the back. To try and make it look more like an evening dress, Mum covered it in pink net. Looking back, it must have looked horrendous! But off I went to join Gerry and his friends.

This time I noticed that the table near the stage was occupied by several young people. This time, we all danced to an orchestra, everyone looked lovely, even the men in their bow ties.

As the evening was coming to a close, another young man entered the room. He went over and spoke to his friends near the stage. Then suddenly, he was beside me, asking if he could have the last waltz with me. I looked at Gerry, who nodded. I can still remember the feel of his velvet jacket, as Michael took me in his arms. He told me he was home for the weekend as he was in the RAF. He took me home and asked if he could see me the next day.

And so began my romance with Michael, and I looked forward to the weekends, when we either went dancing or to the cinema. I still went on Thursdays to classes with Gerry. On my birthday in December, Gerry bought me a gold chain necklace and bracelet. My mum did not approve, because he was so much older than me. So I hardly wore them, and my Thursday classes soon faded out.

At the next Saturday dance, Mike took me to the table by the stage and introduced me to his friends.

There was Margaret and her fiancé, Dickie, his sister, Diane, and her boyfriend, David. There was another couple, Roy and Julie, and an older chap named Dave, who made us laugh by using words like 'indubitably' and 'salubriously' all the time. Sometimes, a good-looking young man with blond hair would join us. The others called him Humphrey but I preferred the name Bill. He worked in a drawing office, and always had a good supply of pencils, which he would snap in half if he got upset. My dad used to find these afterwards, under the table.

One Saturday, we went to Sanderson Wallpapers; they had had a factory close to Perivale Station. This also had a large dance floor, and a rest room and bar with most unusual wallpaper. However, it didn't have that intimate feel that Hoovers had. We went to each on alternate months. There was always the same crowd, the same band, and Mr and Mrs Heath. I decided to ditch the bridesmaid's dress – Mike thought the buckle at the back odd – and I had enough money to buy a new one.

I got a bus to Ealing, and fell in love with a dress in the window. It was ballerina length, strapless and red! It had two layers of net over nylon and it fitted like a dream. It also went with my dark hair. That evening, I wore it to Sanderson's and got a lot of admiring looks – though not from the girls! Later that evening, there was a fight going on in the entrance hall, apparently over me!

Mike and Humphrey had come to blows, and Mike won. However, our romance was short-lived. Mike then met another girl, and they had to get married as she was pregnant.

It was about this time that I joined the Perivale Operatic Society. They regularly performed Gilbert and Sullivan operettas at Hoovers and were very popular.

The rehearsals were held at the Scout hall, near Perivale Station, at the bottom of Horsenden Hill. Nervously I went along, and was considered good enough to join the contraltos; being able to read music helped. Mike's mum was there, along with Margaret and others I knew from dancing.

We each had a libretto of *Iolanthe*, and some had *Trial by Jury*. Connie Reid played the piano as well as taking us through our parts. We all met on Friday evenings, and later on we spent most of Sundays on stage at Hoovers. I absolutely loved it.

During this time, I was working at British Waxed Wrappings, designing here bread wrappers and sweet wrappers. This was at Neasden, North London. As you left the station, BWW was a large modern building across the road. On the ground floor were the printing machines, and on the first floor were the offices and a very large studio at the end.

My boss was Mr Vandy, a large, lumbering man. He sat at the back of the room (so that he could keep an eye on us!).

At his drawing board, in front of Mr Vandy, sat Guy, then me, then Josie, with Ursula at the front. Gill joined us later on and sat on the other side. We all designed and painted the wrappers, and Ursula did the black and white artwork ready for printing. The bread wrappers were for all over the world, so there was plenty of work. When they were being printed, we could go downstairs and watch our work coming off the machines, which was always exciting especially when we saw the multicoloured sweet papers produced. I used to feel quite upset if I saw someone unwrap and throw away their sweet wrapper without even looking at it.

As a team, we all got on very well, and we had lots of fun whenever Mr Vandy – or 'Lumberlegs' as Josie called him – left the room.

Alan

At one of the Saturday dances at Hoovers, another young man had joined our table. He was a friend of Roy's, and was also the only son of Reg and Dorothy Heath. He was quite nice looking, with wavy dark auburn hair. As neither of us had a partner, we soon became an item. He had just returned from Korea, and had served in the Military Police. His mum and dad were obviously very proud of him.

So began our friendship. He had a great sense of humour and we loved going to the pictures to see comedies which starred Peter Sellers. One of our favourites was *Monsieur Hulot's Holiday* with Jacques Tati.

We also went for walks on Sundays, and sometimes I was invited to lunch at Alan's house in Wrysdale Crescent, Perivale. We would sit in the garden, or listen to music. However, I still had rehearsals to go to, and later on, Alan would come and watch when we rehearsed at Hoovers.

Iolanthe was a huge success and I loved every minute of it. We performed every night for a week and it was difficult to get tickets, especially on the last night, when all the principals received bouquets, especially Connie Reid, for all her hard work. There was a full orchestra, and the costumes and scenery were all hired, so the whole production was very professional.

I don't remember saying goodbye to Windmill Lane, my home for fifteen years, but suddenly a house became available near the Hoover factory. It was a semi-detached, three-bedroomed house in Bideford Avenue, Perivale. We were on a bus route and quite close to the station. In fact, the railway embankment ran alongside, but we soon got used to the noise.

There were a few shops close by, also a lovely little church, a park and a pub. Mum busied herself furnishing the new home and tending the gardens, back and front.

I found it much easier to get to work, as I could get the bus

Clara Boor née Read.

Caroline Howlett née Cushion with Phyllis and Lenny.

John Howlett with his prize bull.

Nana Howlett in her garden in Bungay.

Phyllis Howlett with her pet goat.

Going for a stroll at Pakefield 1938–39.

Me at two-and-a-half years.

My junior high school photograph.

Me, Mum and a friend.

My dad in his Bedford truck on the quayside at Lowestoft with the fishing fleet in the background, 1933–4.

Mum, Dad and me at the back of 89 Windmill Lane.

Me in my ballet dress, ten years old.

Phyllis and Gordon on Lowestoft Promenade.

Dad in the garden at 89 Windmill Lane.

Gordan Arthur Read joining the Fire Service.

Mum and Dad sharing a joke with Maisie in her back garden.

Dad, Mum , me – thirteen years – with Uncle Marcus at Lowestoft.

*Me in the Mikado,
February 1956.*

*Going to the dance in my
turquoise evening dress.
The back garden in
Perivale.*

Beside the River Brent, Greenford.
Seventeen years old.

*Mum with Timmy
in the garden at 30
Bideford Avenue.*

*Mum and Dad
in Bungay.*

Mum at the lodge in Buxmoor, Hemel Hempstead.

Mum and Dad's house at Gadebridge, Hemel Hempstead.

*Alan and me with
Tinker at Perivale.*

*Alan in the park,
Greenford.*

*Alan and me on
our wedding day,
22 June 1956.*

*At Boxmoor, with Auntie Simone, Nana Boor, my parents and
Alan. I was three months pregnant.*

from across the road to Alperton Station. There I would change to one going to Wembley, then get a train to the next stop, which was Neasden. This was fine unless there was a football match on at Wembley; then I had a job getting on a bus!

The only thing that spoiled the move was that Tinker went missing for several days. I was so upset that Mum went and bought a little ginger kitten and called it Timmy. This was no consolation and I hardly looked at it. Several more days passed before Tinker put in an appearance. He was walking along the six-foot fence that separated us from the car park. He looked as if he had a droopy moustache, but it turned out to be a grass snake in his mouth! I was overjoyed to see him – though not the grass snake that he so proudly brought us! – and then I accepted Timmy. Unfortunately, Tinker didn't! But eventually they became friends, and all was well at 30 Bideford Avenue.

On our first Easter together, Alan and I went with his parents, Reg and Dorothy, down to Brighton. We all stayed with Vera and Bill, who had a small high-rise flat there. Vera had stayed with Alan's parents during the war, on directed labour, while Bill was in the navy. Years later, Vera told me that Dorothy had asked what sandwiches she could make for her to pack up. Vera said that she didn't mind, and perhaps some peanut butter ones. Dorothy then made her peanut butter sandwiches *every day*! I got on with them both, even though they were about twenty years or more older than me.

Bill was great fun. When we arrived, we could hear him singing 'Stranger in Paradise'. He had fixed a record player into the frame of a chair, and was playing Tony Bennett's recording. This was played many times, and that tune had special memories for both of us.

Because the flat had only one bedroom, I had to share a double bed with Dorothy and Vera. I had to sleep in the middle, which wasn't very comfortable, as they were both much larger than me! Alan, Reg and Bill had sleeping bags on the front room floor. We went for walks around Brighton during the day, and played cards in the evening. There was lots of laughter and I really enjoyed our holiday. It was the start of a lasting relationship with Vera and Bill.

We all settled down to life in Perivale. In the summer we got engaged. Mum and I put on a special meal, which we had with Dorothy and Reg, and I even made individual place menus. Alan and I had gone up to London and bought a Bravington ring, then walked along the Embankment, where Alan proposed to me, opposite City Hall. On the way back home, I couldn't help but keep glancing at my hand, and wondered if the other passengers on the train knew that we had just got engaged...

Alan would often come and sit with us to watch the TV, which Mum had got from Radio Rentals. We particularly liked *Top of the Pops* and Spike Milligan, though Mum and Dad didn't.

In the autumn, we started dancing again, and rehearsals began for *The Mikado*. This time Alan joined.

Things were changing within our group. Dave Garforth, who was older than all of us and lived opposite me, threw a party. His parents went out, and let us have the run of the house. Dave emptied the front room and cleverly draped the ceiling with crepe paper, to great effect. There was plenty to eat and drink and lively music to dance to. I had gone into the kitchen to get something to eat, when Dickie, followed me in and grabbed hold of me and kissed me hard. I was flustered and shocked, especially as he was engaged to be married soon. Embarrassed, I returned to the dancing. Julie and Roy had gone upstairs.

At one of the Sanderson dances, we were all sitting in the rest room having a drink. Diane, who had married David, got up to go to the ladies. She had been rather a long time so I went to find her. She was still in one of the cubicles, moaning and crying; she had had a miscarriage and needed help. I went back to the others and someone called for an ambulance while we tried to console her. Unfortunately, after that she was unable to have any children.

The next bombshell was Roy and Julie, who had to get married. Alan's mum, who had a very Victorian attitude to life, was horrified. So we had to be very careful not to get carried away! This was very difficult for us at times, as we were engaged for nearly two years. We were saving hard and buying things for our 'bottom drawer'. Alan had a job at Pond's and wasn't earning very much money in the accounts department. His mum and dad wanted to convert the top half of their house so that we could live there, but I didn't like this idea. So my parents said we could have the use of their front room and my bedroom, when we got married, until we found somewhere to live.

This caused a lot of bad feeling all round, and I called the whole thing off, and gave him his ring back. Alan was so unhappy that Reg and Dorothy came round to our house for a chat with my parents, and we decided to get together again. Alan decided to try to get into the Police Force so that we could get a house.

Meanwhile, we continued with the *Mikado* rehearsals, and on Sundays, to break up the session, we would go back to Mum's and have tea, then go back to Hoovers.

The Mikado was a huge success and we got rave reviews in the local paper. The wigs and kimonos had been hired, also the scenery, and we had an excellent orchestra. We had been on stage every night for a week. On the last night, bouquets were handed out to Connie Reid and all the principals, and to my surprise, there was one for me from Alan's mum and dad.

Rehearsals began for *The Gondoliers*, but we didn't continue with it for some reason.

Dorothy and Reg took us to lots of other dances in the area. At one time, we put on our finery and all went to Earl's Court to a big old-time night, hosted by Sidney Thompson, which was broadcast live on the radio. I bought a lovely turquoise dress that had white broderie anglaise flowers scattered on the skirt and bodice. These had diamantés in the centre that caught the lights from the glitter ball as it turned.

Some weekends they took us to meet various members of their family. This was when Reg didn't have to go to London to learn new dances. They had a very busy social life. Reg was an export manager at CAV, and he drove a big Wolseley car, which he sometimes let Alan use.

The Wedding

During our long engagement, we managed to see a few concerts and shows, as well as films, even though we were saving up.

I remember seeing Daniel Barenboim playing Beethoven's *Emperor* Concerto, at the Festival Hall on the Embankment.

We went to see *Kismet* at the Stoll Theatre (the stage version) with its wonderful music by Rimsky-Korsakov, especially our tune, Stranger in Paradise.

We went to cinemas up in London as well as the local ones. We saw *Trapeze* at Tottenham Court Road. Alan liked Gina Lollobrigida, and I liked Tony Curtis. We later enjoyed all the Bond movies as they came out.

The date was set for 22 June 1956, at Perivale Parish Church.

I had seen a film starring Mitzi Gaynor in which she wore a dress that I thought would look wonderful for my wedding day.

Dorothy had all her evening dresses made by a designer who lived in Acton. She took me along to meet her, and I sketched out what I wanted. It had a stand away neckline that went into a deep V at the back, finishing with a bow.

I went to John Lewis in London, and found some heavy white embossed satin that looked suitable.

I went for several fittings, and on one occasion, the designer had a small black and white television on, and I watched Maria Callas singing *Tosca*. Very moving and memorable.

Alan and I had bought some Stag bedroom furniture, which we placed in my bedroom, and a few pieces for the front room, which we got in a sale at Times Furnishing, Watford.

We had previously bought three rug kits, which we had completed in the evenings.

The invitations had been sent, flowers ordered and the banns read, so all was ready.

On 22 June, I was awake early, got dressed and went shopping up the road for Mum. It was a gorgeous summer day, and I was very calm. I put on my wedding dress, and it fitted like a dream. I came down the stairs to where my dad was waiting, looking more nervous than me. It was just a small drive to the little church across the way. I had two little bridesmaids: Carol, who was Maisie's daughter, and Diane, who was a daughter of a fireman friend of Dad's. Mum had made their dresses, which were powder blue organza, and they looked very pretty.

After the service, we all went into the nearby park for the photographs.

As well as a few family (mostly on Alan's side) and friends, all of my work mates from BWW came, as well as a couple who worked with Alan. Vera and Bill also came from Brighton.

After the reception at the Myllet Arms, we went home to change. I had bought a dress and jacket in a little shop in Neasden. It was deep blue glazed cotton, with tiny white flowers printed on it. I wore a little white hat, white gloves and white stiletto shoes, all very fashionable at the time. Alan's dad let us borrow his car for our honeymoon, and after saying our good-byes, we set off for Swanage in Dorset. We didn't go very far before we removed the items tied to the back of the Wolseley, and the kippers from inside the engine!

Early Days

The drive to Swanage, in Dorset, was very long, and we didn't arrive at the hotel until after midnight.

Everything was in darkness, but someone came to let us in and show Alan where to park the car. Then we were shown upstairs to our room. We tried to be quiet while we unpacked our cases, but on opening the wardrobe door, we found it was filled with metal coat hangers that jangled together, making such a noise that we went into fits of laughter. I put on my new nightdress. It was rose pink, and because it was see-through, I had sewn some pink cotton fabric underneath it to hide my embarrassment. Alan went into the bathroom and changed into his pyjamas.

We got into bed, had a kiss and a cuddle and suddenly he was on top of me, and it was all over!

He quickly fell asleep, but I lay there in the dark, for ages. Is this what we have been waiting for? I asked myself. Feeling damp and uncomfortable, I eventually fell asleep.

Aware of the sunlight in our bedroom, we both woke up and wondered what the time was. There was no clock in the room, and Alan's watch had stopped. We couldn't hear a sound in the hotel so we thought everyone must be downstairs. We quickly got washed and dressed and went downstairs. A cleaner was doing the stairs, and looked at us in amazement! We said, 'Good morning,' and as we passed her I glanced at the wall clock. It was half past five!

We made out that we were going for a walk, and quickly made our exit. Luckily it was a glorious morning and we made our way to the beach and walked along the promenade. After a very long stroll, we returned and found that all the other residents were sitting at breakfast. We obviously looked like newlyweds, as the other married couples glanced at us with knowing smiles.

'Your table, Mr and Mrs *Heat!*' the waiter mispronounced. Nervously, we sat down and I realised that I had never poured him out a cup of tea before, and didn't know how much sugar he took.

After breakfast, we went upstairs to freshen up. In the hallway was a table with a bowl of lilies on it, and their perfume still takes me back to that time. We explored Swanage. It was lovely, as was the weather; but looking back, it was more like a holiday than a honeymoon.

One day we drove to Studland Bay. I had packed a picnic and we spent the day on the beach. What we didn't realise was that the sun sets behind you. We got up to leave and I felt very ill. Alan got me into the car as quickly as he could and drove back to the hotel. I had sunstroke and was shivering a lot. He got me into bed and placed lots of blankets and an eiderdown on top of me and left me to sleep. I recovered, but my neck was very red and sore.

One evening after our meal, we went and played miniature golf in a park opposite the hotel. I got a lot of funny looks as I had on my white stiletto heels. Anyway, I enjoyed the game, and even got a hole in one, which brought a round of applause from the spectators.

And so, after a disappointing week romantically, we made the long journey back home to settle down as Mr and Mrs Heath.

We quickly settled into a routine when we got back to Perivale. I enjoyed my job at BWW and Alan was still at Pond's. We still went dancing, and going to the pictures, and started learning *The Pirates of Penzance*.

We had the use of the front room, but to save on coal, Mum usually asked us into the back when we came home from work. I was also getting annoyed, as she would very often have our evening meal cooked for us. She couldn't understand that I wanted to do things for myself. If I did, she would make a point of clearing up behind me. Mum was the dominant one. She made all the decisions and did all the decorating. My dad was the quiet one, and just sat back and let her get on with things. She never showed me how to cook. When I got the chance, I referred to cookery books for something special. She also thought she was helping us by doing our washing and ironing, so I felt pretty useless, and on top of all this our love life was pretty non-existent.

Nevertheless, after nearly two years, I managed to become pregnant.

I was overjoyed, and confided in Josie my friend at work. This turned out to be a good move, as she was about to get married to Dave and had suddenly got chickenpox! She was off work when she telephoned BWW and asked if she could speak to me; this didn't go down very well with Mr Vandy. She had been asked by her doctor if she had been in contact with anyone who was pregnant. If she had, I was to get an injection straight away, to protect the baby. I then had to tell Mr Vandy that I was pregnant, and could I please have time off to go to the doctor's?

He immediately agreed, and I went for the jab. Of course I was very worried, but the doctor thought as it was early days I should be all right. I was very upset that I couldn't go to Josie's wedding, as I was told not to get in contact with her yet.

Meanwhile, Alan was taking exams to get into the Police Force. He managed to pass them all, but he was overweight and they gave him six weeks to lose several pounds. He cut out sugar, bread and potatoes and managed to reach his target in time.

He then went to Witney, Oxfordshire, to a police training college.

I had continued working, but I was blooming and finding it more difficult to get near the drawing board! Suddenly, there was a bus strike. I knew one of the printers lived near me, and he offered me a lift. What I didn't know was that he had a motorbike and sidecar...

With great difficulty, I managed to squeeze myself into the sidecar, and off we went down the Western Avenue. I felt as if I was sitting on the ground, especially when we were alongside a bus! However, I survived this mode of transport until the strike was over. I also managed to work right up until the end so as to claim maternity benefit.

Changes

E arly one Saturday morning, I was woken up by the sounds of Mum and Dad having a terrible row. I was on my own, as Alan was away, and I lay there listening to Mum's voice getting louder and louder. Suddenly she appeared in my room, in a very distressed state. 'Go and talk some sense into your father,' she said. 'He says he is leaving me!'

I heaved myself and the bump out of the bed and went into their bedroom. My mother went downstairs, sobbing.

Dad was dressed and packing things into a suitcase. I then realised this was serious. I didn't know what to say to him; he seemed determined and avoided looking at me.

I managed to ask him questions like, 'What do you think you are doing?' and 'Where are you going?' But all he said was, 'You don't know what she's like' – meaning my mum. I left the room, realising that I didn't really know my parents.

My quiet father had found another woman!

He left the house, a sad figure in a raincoat.

Mum was hysterical by this time and I couldn't console her.

I got washed and dressed and found the nearest phone box and telephoned Alan in Witney. We had managed to buy an old car so that he could come home some weekends.

After I explained what had happened, he returned home.

I tried to get Mum to have a cup of tea, but to no avail. Alan eventually arrived and he tried to comfort her, but she just sobbed and sobbed. I decided to make dinner for us all. I found some sausages and made toad-in-the-hole, but of course she wouldn't touch it.

Later, when she calmed down, she told us that 'the other woman' worked in Hoovers, and from her description I realised I had seen her talking to my dad, at the gatehouse. Nothing much to look at, and she had thick legs.

Somehow we got through Sunday, and Alan went back to

Witney. On Monday, Dad came back. I think he had a guilt complex and couldn't go through with it. Mum had said that she would never take him back, but of course she did. We all tried to behave as if nothing had happened, but it was a bit like walking on eggshells.

I had left work and in November the birth was imminent. Alan came home the weekend the baby was due, but nothing happened. The next weekend he didn't come, but on Saturday night the baby decided to! I had gone to the bathroom about two o'clock and Mum heard me. Even though I told her it wasn't yet, she still went and called an ambulance. Everyone kept asking me how often the pains were and I didn't know.

At Acton Hospital, more questions until the morning, then I was prepared and taken up to the Labour Ward, where women were in various stages of labour, and moaning. I wasn't. Alan appeared for a short while, but he had to go back. Brian Anthony arrived later that evening, but I hardly remember it as I was so drugged up.

When I opened my eyes, I was in a small room by myself.

Almost immediately a nurse entered the room carrying a small bundle. Silently, she placed this tiny baby in my arms and left.

I couldn't take my eyes off this lovely little boy that I had produced. He only weighed 6 lb 12 oz, and I wished that Alan was here with me, to see his son.

The nurse returned. 'Haven't you fed him yet?' she asked.

Now I never went to antenatal classes because I was working, but I knew my milk hadn't come yet. Nobody had told me that you still had to put baby to the breast. The bossy nurse showed me what to do, then marched out of the room.

Later, I was moved to a general ward with other mums. On the third day my milk arrived with a vengeance. I produced so much it had to be expressed, which was very painful! Apparently it is stored and used to feed other babies. In America, you get paid for doing this.

About this time, the baby blues set in. I cried a lot, and I was missing Alan. Everyone thought I was a single mother.

In those days, you had to stay in hospital for ten days. I had to beg to be allowed home on the ninth day as it was my twenty-first birthday. As all seemed well with both of us, they agreed, and Dorothy and Reg arrived to take us home. Dorothy was annoyed that I wouldn't let her carry my baby in the car.

When we arrived at Bideford Avenue, they all took turns holding him, with lots of 'oohs' and 'aahs'. He needed a feed and they left so that I could be alone with him in peace.

I looked around the front room, with its mixture of baby and twenty-first cards, which Mum had put round. There were a lot of baby clothes, presents and nappies etc. I had a lovely mother-of-pearl powder compact that played *La vie en rose*, from my parents, and a bouquet of flowers from Alan's parents.

Later that evening, my friend Diane called in to see me and Brian. She had been told that she would not be able to conceive after her miscarriage. We chatted for a while and looked at all the cards and presents before she left me alone with my son. This then, was my twenty-first birthday, 10 December 1958.

Two weeks before Brian was born, we had a letter from Vera in Brighton, to let us know that she had just given birth to Michael and he was 10 lb! This came as a huge surprise, as they had been married for ten years and had given up trying. Vera was a big built woman, and she had no idea that she was pregnant. She had gone to the doctor's complaining of backache. When she got home and tearfully told Bill, he fell about laughing! They had to leave their flat and go into a council house. I didn't reply straight away as they didn't know I was expecting, so I wrote back and said 'Snap!' We now had something in common, which brought us even closer together.

Brian was difficult to feed; I could not satisfy him, even though I had plenty of milk. However, I persevered for six months. I felt very proud pushing him up the shops in the grey Pedigree pram, and quickly got into the routine of bathing, changing and feeding. I would put him outside in the garden all weathers, after wrapping him up well.

Of course his grandparents spoiled him, and I think it helped to bring my parents a bit closer together.

New Beginnings

Meanwhile, Alan had passed all his exams and was officially a police constable. We had to wait now to see where we were being posted. I remember clearly the day we heard that we were going to Hemel Hempstead in Hertfordshire.

We were elated, but Mum couldn't contain her tears. She would be losing us and her beautiful grandson. She would be alone with my dad and the painful silence that would descend.

We started packing things up and we left Perivale, with our few pieces of furniture in a van, and Brian in his carrycot in the back of our old car.

We arrived at 241 Turner's Hill, a semi-detached house in the middle of a group of eight. They were fairly new and had very long front and back gardens. Hemel was a new and sprawling town and our house was on the top of one of the hills. There was a very steep descent down to the town and the Police Station. Halfway along was the West Herts Hospital, where apparently I had been sent when I was about five, to have my tonsils removed.

Hemel had some lovely stores, especially Sainsbury's; there was also a very large open market, but I did find it a bit difficult pushing the pram uphill!

We soon settled down to our new life, and as Brian was six months old, I started him on a bottle and introduced baby food. He was much happier now and soon got used to his own room. I bought an electric sewing machine and made all the curtains, some cheap dresses for me and even baby clothes. When I wasn't knitting or sewing there was always gardening to be done. Dorothy and Reg bought us a dozen rose bushes, which we put on one side of the front path. The other side was lawn with a border all round. After I put Brian to bed, I would busy myself weeding, especially when Alan was at work. At first he seemed quite happy with the shifts, which were 6 a.m.–2 p.m., 2 p.m.–

10 p.m. and nights which were 10 p.m.–6 a.m. After three weeks of shift work he then had a week off. Some days he had court duty. The pay wasn't very good because we were given accommodation. We were expected to keep the gardens looking nice and the decorating in good order, so there was always plenty to do. Alan attempted to do some wallpapering – with disastrous results!

I decided to get help from the sergeant who lived next door to us. When he saw the front room wall, he said that the paper would all have to come off as it wasn't straight. He then made him a plumb line and showed Alan what to do. After that it was plain sailing.

We had some local shops nearby, and most days I would push the pram up the road. The clinic and doctor's surgery were also there. One day, I called in at the butcher's, came out and walked halfway round the square before I realised that I had left Brian outside the shop! When he was a little older and sitting up, I had bought most of the shopping, but couldn't fit a bottle of bleach into the bag, so I stood it upright at the bottom of the pram. When I came out of the chemist's, to my horror Brian had the lid in his hand. I panicked and ran back into the chemist's to ask for advice in case he had got any in his mouth. Luckily, he wasn't sick and all was well.

We hadn't been at Turner's Hill very long, when one day I had an unexpected visit from the Chief Constable. He came in and asked me how we liked living here. He said that large groups of police houses didn't always work out as everyone knew what the other was earning, and it could cause a bit of jealousy if one had something more than another. I said that so far we were getting on well with everybody and that we loved living here.

One morning, we were very surprised to find that the sergeant, his wife and two daughters had done a moonlight flit! In the night, they had completely emptied the house, and nobody heard or saw a thing. Later on we learned that they had gone to Australia.

We had been living at Turner's Hill a while and I wanted another baby. I didn't want Brian to be an only child as I had been. We were not successful at first (things were still difficult in that department), but eventually I fell. I absolutely bloomed this time, and was pleased to hear that I could have a home birth.

And so on 11 March 1961, Kevin Andrew was born, weighing in at 7 lb 12 oz. The midwife only liked girls, and I will never forget her holding him up, and saying, 'Not another bloody boy!'

My mother had just had a hysterectomy, but she still insisted on coming and helping me.

They had both moved over to Hemel, as Dad had lost his job and of course the house as a result of his 'affair'. At first they got a job running an off-licence at Bury St Edmunds and living over the shop, but that was very hard work and didn't last long. So they advertised in our local paper, as they wanted to be near me, and got a reply from a couple who felt sorry for them and were willing to share their house.

And so it was that they suddenly appeared on our doorstep one day, on their way to see Doris and Fred. They had put their furniture into storage for the time being.

Luckily they all got on, and Mum and Dad went to stay with them. It wasn't long before they saw an advert requiring a housekeeper and handyman, with live-in accommodation. They applied and got the jobs and went to live in Boxmoor, just outside Hemel. They moved into the gatehouse, which was very quaint. Mum worked very hard up at the big house and was often at work until late in the evening, cooking and serving at dinner parties.

It was while she was there that she became so ill that she had to have her womb removed. They then got onto the housing list, as it was impossible for her to carry on in her employment.

As soon as Kevin was born I decided to bottle-feed him. It made such a difference knowing how much he had taken, and neither of us was stressed.

We had him christened in the nearby church. Both sets of grandparents were there, and Alan's cousin Anne and her husband Peter were godparents, along with Vera and Bill, who came up from Brighton with Michael.

It was a lovely day and I even wore a hat, which I made especially for the occasion.

After that we had several holidays with the boys. When Kevin was about six months old and Brian nearly two, we went to Hayling Island holiday camp. Looking back, it might have been where they made *Hi-Di-Hi*, as I recognised some of the settings. Brian loved it, there was lots for him to do, and staff were on hand to mind the little ones if you wanted a break or to watch a show in the evenings.

I didn't like queuing up for my meals, and the chalets were not very clean. In fact the boys kept cleaner on the grass than inside on the floor.

The highlight of the holiday was Kevin winning the bonniest baby competition, and Brian a second prize in the toddlers.

When they got older we took to the water, and had several holidays on the Broads, getting a better boat each time. But there was no romance between Alan and me.

Back on the beat, crime was getting so bad that policemen had to patrol in pairs. Just before we moved to our house, a policeman who used to live next but one to us was attacked in the town and died from head injuries, leaving a wife and four young children. She was later rehoused, and then a young couple moved in. He was very tall and good-looking. He used to call in and have a cup of coffee with me and loved to see the boys. He would walk his Alsatian, called Rocky, past the house every day, and I found myself looking forward to seeing him. I knew I should not have these feelings, and nothing ever came of our relationship; I just enjoyed the attention.

Another holiday we had, while the boys were young, was when Alan's parent took us all down to North Devon. We stayed in a lovely Victorian house called Foxdown, at Buck's Cross. It was close to the sea and surrounded by trees with a stream trickling by. The weather was glorious and we went to some beautiful places, like Hartland Point and Clovelly. The only thing was, as it was so hilly it affected my breathing. On one occasion, Reg was driving us somewhere, and suddenly he couldn't breathe. I told him to stop the car, and I got into the seat beside him and managed to get him to take a couple of puffs from my inhaler. It brought immediate relief, and from that day he had to have treatment.

One evening, after our meal, I had an upset stomach. The next day, I felt so bad that Alan and his parents took the boys out for the day and left me in bed. Later on I felt a bit better, so I dressed and made my way to the kitchen for a drink. The owner's son was preparing the evening meal and was glad of someone to talk to. He was also the waiter, and obviously enjoyed his food by the look of him. I sat and chatted to him in this huge old kitchen, and he invited me to a party on the beach later that evening. I told Alan about it when they returned, and he didn't want to go but said I could. So after our meal, I put the boys to bed and set off with the waiter in his sports car. In the dark, we drove down lanes to the beach. You could hear the waves but could not see anything. We walked onto the sand and joined a small group of people sitting round a fire. Everyone had brought a bottle of something and we had a bottle of champagne.

It was such a new experience for me, laughing and talking to people, sitting here in the dark on the beach. I felt exhilarated, and also a little chilly, so my friend put his jacket around my shoulders. Couples started kissing and cuddling and we decided to make our way back to Foxdown. Years later, I realised that he was gay, but at the time I didn't know of such things. Needless to say, I got a frosty reception from the in-laws next morning. We were there for two weeks, and in all that time Alan and I never had sex.

One of our most memorable holidays was with Vera, Bill and Michael, when we hired a larger craft on the Broads. We never stopped laughing the entire holiday. For one thing the boat was difficult to navigate, especially under bridges. Then there was the time we ran aground one night near Yarmouth. We had put the boys to bed in their sleeping bags, and we were playing cards. Suddenly we noticed that the money was rolling off the table, then all the cupboards on one side flew open and the crockery fell out!

While Vera and I cleared up – walking at an angle and laughing – Alan and Bill went outside, and in the dark tried to straighten up the boat, to no avail. The tide was going out at Breyden Water, so it was decided that it was best left until morning when the craft would right itself. We looked in at the lads who were still asleep, even though they were in a heap. The next morning, as expected, the boat had righted itself and we set off to Stalham.

Once there, we moored and Bill took Alan and the boys out in a sailing dinghy. Vera and I stood on the bank taking photographs, when suddenly the boom swung round and hit Bill on the head! Luckily he was all right, but it caused a lot of amusement.

At one time we went down to Brighton for a break, and we took our Jack Russell, Patch, along. *Big mistake.* He didn't like travelling in the car, and we had to keep stopping to give him a walk. Then one night, he wouldn't settle so we tied his lead to a dining chair, only to find in the morning that he had chewed up everything in sight, including the chair!

Alan was getting very moody and more bad-tempered. It was considered that he might be happier on another beat. So we all moved onto the nearby estate of Bennetts End. We had one of the older police houses and he was to be the 'local bobby'. Patch, our dog, managed to clear the back fence and got run over. His legs were longer than most and they got very badly injured, but he survived. The cat we had at Turner's Hill found its way back across two main roads and finished up, living wild in the fields behind where we used to live.

Our move brought no improvement to Alan's temper. The locals knew where he lived and slashed the tyres of our car one night. (It stood at the front of the house.) One evening he was checking the local shops, and his bike was taken and thrown over some hedges round a playing field. He came home, ran upstairs and would not speak to me. I didn't know about it until a groundsman brought it back to me, after looking in the saddlebag. He wanted to leave the force but his Chief Constable suggested that a move to Tring would make life a lot easier.

Meanwhile, my parents had been allocated a council house at Gadebridge, Hemel Hempstead. Dad was employed at Rotax, and Mum had got a job as a cook at the Police Station. She enjoyed it there. The officers were always playing tricks on her and her helper, Jean. On one occasion someone tied a firework to the back of Mum's apron. Unfortunately, it burnt her leg and clothing and she had to go to A&E! Another time, they put flour into the fan so when she switched it on she got covered in flour.

It was while she was there that she took her driving test. Fortunately she passed, and was very relieved as she knew that they would be watching her from the windows. There was much laughter one day, when she drove away with a loaf of bread on top of the car.

One day, Jean and she decided to make each other's faces up. Neither of them wore any make-up and wondered if anyone would notice. They served up the teas with their eyes heavily made up and nobody even noticed!

When we still lived in Hemel, I went shopping with her one day. We went to Sainsbury's and were aware of lots of security about. When we got into the crowded store, who should come in but Muhammad Ali! You could not get really close because of his huge minders, but I could see how good-looking he was and what a lovely colour his skin was. He was promoting a night-time drink and was making several quips about Joe Frazier. He defeated him in 1974, so it must have been about that time.

Mum and Dad's house at Butt's End was very nice and they overlooked a large park where Brian and Kevin used to play football later on. Gadebridge was at the edge of Hemel, and the River Gade ran through the town surrounded by trees and lots of grass. This was nice to see, as Hemel was such a large industrial new town.

Tring

I fell in love with Tring straight away. The police house in Grove Road was an old semi-detached one at the end of a row of private houses. We were quite high up and could see the Chiltern Hills from the front. Unusually, the kitchen was situated at the front and the lounge and dining room were at the back looking onto a very long garden. Beyond that and beside the house, there were meadows with horses and cows. A short walk down the hill and round the Pheasant pub would bring you into Tring High Street. There were a couple of antique shops, one of which belonged to John Bly; a lovely church; a small International Stores; lots of little shops and of course the Police Station. This was an old building, which would be closed at night. There were only four or five policemen and the local sergeant, George. He lived next door to us and moved at one speed: slow.

With him lived his wife, her sister and a very slow-moving dog. Further along Grove Road lived Gladys, Roland and their children, with whom I became quite friendly.

We got the boys enrolled into the local school, which looked like something out of a Dickens novel! To get to this, you had to pass the local butcher's shop and the only village store and post office. Very soon I got to know the locals and them me. Alan seemed a lot happier there, as things went at a slower pace, but he still didn't like night work.

We all settled down to our new way of life, including Patch, who loved his new walks. However, we still had a job keeping him in. Alan would get very annoyed when our phone rang to let him know that 'a Jack Russell was worrying their sheep'! He would have to get the police van out, and try to catch him.

During the day, I would attach his lead to the linen line so that he could run up and down the garden – much to the amazement of the horses, who would lean over the fence watching him dash up and down. Sometimes I had to unwind him from the linen post, as he had gone round and round and was nearly choking! I also had to tether him in the kitchen, as he couldn't be trusted in the house. He would chew the boys' Lego, and when left alone, he would start on the mat. One day he had the boys' socks and the crutch out of Alan's pants as they hung on the line!

Alan's parents gave us a heavy oak table which Alan managed to saw in half. With the wood, he made a kennel for Patch, but he even chewed the corners of that! He would get so frustrated with the dog that he would kick him when he was wearing his police boots. This was such a shame, as he was a lovely little character.

One winter, I opened the kitchen curtains and was surprised to see snow halfway up the window! It had blown across from the Chiltern Hills. The front garden had such deep drifts, nobody could get out.

On another occasion, I walked into the kitchen to see a cow looking in through the window. She and her friends had escaped during the night. It caused much amusement to see George the sergeant and a farmer, trying to round them up that morning.

I loved living in Tring, but as the boys got older I was beginning to get bored. So I got a lunchtime job helping out in the kitchen of The Bell in the high street. I helped Wendy the cook with the meals and learned how to do side salads, then there was all the washing-up to do. It was hectic! If we did get a quiet day, the landlady would get Wendy to defrost the fridge and the freezer, and I had to scrub the concrete floor on my hands and knees. I also had to wash all the tea towels. One day, as I was washing-up, I suddenly had a terrific pain between my shoulder blades. I was later diagnosed as having an ulcer and advised to leave my employment. I then started painting and did several dog portraits for the locals. My reputation grew, and one day a local farmer called Duncan came to see me. He had bought a shop close to the Police Station and wanted to sell antiques. He had decided to get rid of a lot of stuff from his house and had gone into partnership with a young lady named Sue, who was interested in buying and selling. Duncan brought me the sign above the shop and wanted me to paint it. It was to be called 'Thyngs Ancient and Modern'. I did the background white with black lettering in Old-English style. He paid me for that, and then asked me if I would like to work in the shop part time. I said I knew nothing about antiques, and jokingly he said, 'Neither do I!' And so I started to work in the mornings for Duncan and Sue.

At first, the shop was set out nicely with some lovely furniture, porcelain and pictures, but that soon changed when Duncan started to fill every available space with mostly house clearance stuff, a lot of it rubbish!

There was also a cellar, which was cold and damp, and a lot of farming stuff and pots and pans went down there.

I met a lot of interesting people while I was there, and gradually started to learn about antiques. However, the trade was open to tricksters, and as I was often alone in the shop they took advantage of my naivety.

One such occasion was when two traders came in and asked if I had any chests of drawers. I knew that Duncan had recently brought in one that was in a bad condition, and had put it in the hallway outside. I couldn't see a price on it and they offered me £30 to take it away. I thought this was all right, and sold it. Duncan was not best pleased that I had sold a £300 bow-fronted chest of draws for £30! I was very upset, but at least he learned to tell me what was what in future. Another time, three people came in together. A man and a woman wanted to know if we wanted to purchase a set of silver spoons. I had to go into the back room to telephone Duncan, who said he would come and look at them. The third man was looking at something in the front window, which had a curtain across halfway down so that it was easy to look over at the items on display. Duncan arrived, and after a discussion he decided not to buy. I then walked over to the window and discovered that a bronze statue was missing! We then realised we were victims of a scam. The man at the window must have leaned over the rail, lifted the bronze and put it in a pocket of his long mac while we were distracted by the other two. Duncan informed the police, who said that they knew about these three. They were working their way down from Aylesbury towards Hemel Hempstead. The woman wore a different-coloured wig at every stop.

We gradually got to know all the dealers and those whom we could trust. Sometimes Sue would be in the shop. She was very beautiful and was married to the local solicitor. He would often pop in for a coffee, as would several of Duncan's family. It was such a friendly atmosphere to work in and, when I had finished my shift, I was relieved by an older woman called Rowena.

One evening I went with Rowena, her husband and son to a good-old-days-type dinner and cabaret in Tring. Several people hired costumes, but I bought a suitable gown from an actress who sold it to Duncan. It was strapless, made of black taffeta and had a bustle at the back. I wore long gloves, a feather boa and a large picture hat. John Bly was the master of ceremonies and we all joined in the singing and had a jolly good time.

Ronnie

One day, the doorbell tinkled and in came this imposing figure of a man called Ronnie. He looked somewhat like Henry VIII. He had long grey hair, moustache and beard, a kindly face and a large stomach, over which he wore a loose blue shirt that matched his eyes. He introduced himself as Ronnie and said, 'Hello, sweetie,' which I learned he called all young ladies.

Ronnie lived on the corner of the High Street and was a very well-known character in Tring and the antiques trade. He went to auctions in his old Morris Traveller and had a very keen eye, especially for porcelain. He didn't think much of Duncan's shop, but called in regularly and we became friends. One day, I was listening to my radio in the shop and there was a modern version of Mozart's Symphony No. 40 in G Minor playing. Ronnie came in, and said that I should hear the real thing, and invited me round after work, also to meet his family.

Nervously I approached this very old property, and as I knocked on the side door, I was greeted by two Staffordshire bull terriers. Ronnie appeared and told me not to be scared, and one word from him and they wandered off, making their way, as we did, through dusty antique furniture and ornaments all about the shop ground floor. We reached the foot of a grubby staircase that led to their living quarters: all very Dickensian.

Upstairs in their living area were old armchairs and a sofa with loose covers and cushions. The two dogs lay in front of a very old brick fireplace. There were lots of books about, and down the end of the long room was a grand piano, covered with a cloth on top of which was various objects, some of them antiques. Bedrooms and a bathroom led off of this room, but the kitchen was downstairs.

Ronnie's wife Penny sat by the fire. She was an attractive woman with dark hair tied back in a bun, from which little wisps of hair escaped. She wore dark-rimmed glasses which gave her a studious appearance. She was well spoken and very intelligent. She made me welcome and made me a mug of coffee.

They had three little children, who looked like angels with dirty faces, and were well behaved. Somehow they managed to run around the antiques without breaking anything!

We talked for a while about my life as a policeman's wife until I had to leave to get home for the boys. They asked me to call in again, anytime.

This was the first of many visits, including an evening meal. The boys had gone to stay at my mum's, as it was holiday time and Alan was on a late shift. Ronnie picked me up from work and drove me down to theirs.

On the ground floor we made our way through to the kitchen. The first thing you saw was a large table, piled high with books, papers and bills. These were pushed aside to make spaces for the dinner plates. These were of pewter (and, I guess, old). On these, Ronnie placed chunks of home-made bread that he had made that morning. Next, he ladled into bowls large pieces of lamb cooked with garlic, and lots of carrots and pearl barley with gravy, in which you dunked your bread. It was delicious, and he had cooked it all.

Ronnie poured himself a large glass of whisky, and I then noticed all the bottles under the sink. I soon learned that he drank about a bottle a day. Penny insisted we left the dishes, and we took our drinks (coffee and whisky) upstairs, where Ronnie promptly fell asleep on the sofa. I thought I should leave, but Penny wouldn't hear of it, so I watched her bath the children and put them to bed. We chatted until Ronnie woke up.

He gave me a drink (I think it was whisky and lemonade) and then we talked more seriously. Penny remained in the room as the conversation turned to sex.

He wasn't surprised when I revealed that Alan and I seldom had sex; he said it showed in my eyes. I said that I had tried to 'turn him on' by wearing sexy underwear, but nothing worked. I knew there was a problem and had asked him to see a doctor but he refused. I had already been to see one, who had put me on Valium and asked to see Alan. The doctor also advised me to have a cigarette – which I did! Now and again I would have a Menthol one, as I didn't care much for the other kind. Ronnie did not approve of smoking. (Pity he didn't think the same about drinking.)

It was getting very late, and Ronnie wasn't in a fit state to drive, so it was suggested that I stay the night. Ronnie phoned Alan and told him that I would be home in the morning. Penny made up a bed in the spare room and we all turned in. I couldn't get to sleep for a long while. It was a strange room with odd pieces of furniture covered with sheets. It was eerie and dusty and the bed wasn't very comfortable. I had just closed my eyes, when I heard scurrying sounds above me! As it was such an old building I thought it must be rats.

When I woke up in the morning after what seemed like a short sleep, I told Penny about the noise overhead. 'Oh, that's all right,' she said, 'they are Glis Glis, a small rodent that goes from loft to loft in old buildings.' Apparently these edible dormice are peculiar to the Beaconsfield and Tring area, and there are specimens of them in Tring Museum in Akeman Street, down the road from Thyngs Ancient and Modern.

Penny ran me a bath and then I went downstairs to where Ronnie made me a coffee. He had been up early making bread, as he did every morning. He had wonderfully big strong arms and hands perfect for kneading dough.

Penny took two of the children to school and then came back for me.

Meanwhile, life went on, with Alan getting more and more bad-tempered. He would shout at the boys, and one day he threw their toys out of their bedroom window. He would come home from work, come in the back door, kick the dog and ignore me. I used to stand at the sink and wait for him to hit me, but he never did. Sometimes, when my parents arrived on a Sunday, he would disappear down to the greenhouse for the day. I confided in Mum one day about his behaviour and that he wasn't interested in sex. She was shocked.

One day he came home so angry that he picked up his dinner plate and threw it at the wall! I knew that we couldn't go on like this, we were all so unhappy.

I felt that there must be something wrong with me, the fact that I couldn't 'turn him on'.

Again I went to Ronnie and Penny. He was sure that I was wrong and suggested that I go to Harley Street, to a friend of his who was a gynaecologist.

Ronnie drove me up to London in the Morris Traveller and, feeling nervous, I was shown into a waiting room while Ronnie spoke to his friend. I then had an internal examination which lasted quite a while, and there was a nurse with me all the time. Eventually, I got dressed, while the specialist went to speak with Ronnie. He assured me that there was nothing wrong with me, but stated that he would like to meet my husband. I wasn't sure how I was going to do this, but I told Alan where I had been and that he wanted to see me again. And so I got him to drive up there, and when we got inside, the gynaecologist called Alan in.

He wasn't in there very long, and when I was taken to one side the specialist said that Alan would never be any good for me. We went back home in silence. Ronnie had paid for all this help.

Decisions

I went to see Richard, the solicitor (Sue's husband), to ask about grounds for divorce. He asked me some very embarrassing questions about physical penetration during sex, and how often it took place. Then he asked me if I had had an orgasm. I said that I didn't even know what it meant. Then he asked me if I thought that Alan might be homosexual. I said that I didn't think so, he just wasn't interested in sex. Alan refused to see a doctor, and would walk out of the room if I tried to discuss the problem with him.

Richard then talked about money and how would I manage with the boys, who were about ten and twelve. Where would we live? I left his office with my mind in a whirl; there was so much to think about. I needed to get away.

I got in touch with Vera, my friend in Brighton, and asked her if I could come down on my own, and stay for a few days. Of course she said I could.

And so, with Alan's agreement, I got the train to Brighton. Beforehand I had saved every penny I could. Ronnie had given me some old painted furniture to restore and had paid me well. Also, I made notes of everything in the house that I had bought.

I arrived at Brighton Station and found the bus that would take me up to the estate where Vera and Bill and Michael lived.

Later that evening, I explained the reason for my visit and why I needed time to think. Naturally they were shocked, but not surprised, as Vera knew Alan as a boy and he would suddenly have a tantrum, lie on the floor, kick his legs and smash his toys.

I stayed in Brighton for about a week. I visited the Lanes and looked at the antique shops there, and walked along the seafront. I even walked to Rottingdean one day and sat with my back against the sea wall, looking at the waves. I never spoke to anyone and nobody bothered me. It seemed strange that a woman could walk about on her own and not be accosted, especially at the seaside.

Then one wet afternoon, I decided to go to the cinema. *Ryan's Daughter* was showing, starring Robert Mitchum and Sarah Miles. The place was half full as I took my seat in the stalls. I was completely absorbed in the story and quickly saw a comparison between my life and that of the schoolmaster's wife in the film. Tears were running down my face, and I hoped nobody could see me crying. Somehow I got through the rest of the film, which I thought was very well done. The Irish scenery, the storm and the music were unforgettable, and John Mills was excellent in the part he played.

It was still raining when I stepped outside.

I sat on top of the bus, soaking wet, drained of emotion and still crying. Vera was amazed when she saw the state I was in. I explained about the film and that I had made a decision. Looking back, I realise that film was the turning point in my life.

I went back to Tring and started to make plans for myself and the boys.

The Break-up

When I returned home, I told Alan that I would leave him for good if he didn't go to see a doctor and get some help. He laughed at me and said that I would never leave. Then, refusing to discuss the matter further, he left the room.

His temper got worse and he got rid of Patch, but I don't know how. My health was suffering and I was now on Librium as well as Valium, so the following days were a little hazy.

I know that at sometime I took my parents to meet Ronnie. This was at his request. He thought my dad was 'a poor old boy', and he said I would be better off if I didn't live so near to my mother. On the other hand, they didn't quite know what to make of him – or his living accommodation!

Somehow I managed to find a flat, but I cannot remember how. I told the boys that we were leaving one day, and would they put together the things that they really needed to take with them. I told them that Nanny and Granddad would pick them up at the school gate and they had to wait for them.

And so, one morning when the children had gone to school and Alan was on duty, I quickly started to get things together. My mum and dad arrived to help as planned, as well as Doris and Fred, their friends.

They were all busy loading up their cars, when the telephone rang and I learned that I had lost the flat: I had been gazumped! I was distraught. Quickly, Mum and Doris decided to carry on, and that they would put us up somehow.

What I hadn't realised was that the sergeant who lived next door was at home, and had rung the Police Station to let Alan know that people were removing furniture from his house. Suddenly the police van drew up and Alan stormed down the path. Everyone went and sat in their cars, leaving us alone.

'What the devil's going on?' he shouted.

'I told you I would leave,' I replied. I asked him to look round the house to make sure that I hadn't removed anything of his. This he did, and when he came downstairs, he queried his grandmother's bed. I said it was for one of the boys, and that if he wanted it, we could get it off the top of one of the cars. He then backed down.

I left him sitting dejected on the stairs. We didn't even say goodbye. It was over.

The rest of the day is a bit of a blur. I think we must have gone to Doris's at Crabtree Close, and stored my possessions in their garage. There were the boys' beds, a bed settee, a bookcase and two wall units, some carpet, bedside cabinets a couple of lamps, ornaments, bedding, clothes and my artwork. Mum and Dad drove back to Tring and picked up the boys, as planned, and brought them back to Doris's to be with me. I think they had a few weeks travelling to school by bus before they broke up for the summer holiday.

We stayed with Doris and Fred. The boys slept together in their spare double bed, while I was put in a very tiny box room. However, the boys were not happy there. Doris had painted the outside walls white at the back, and she objected to them kicking a ball about in case it marked them.

One afternoon, I was preparing food in the kitchen, when Brian ran in from the garden. As he ran past me, he swore and started calling me all sorts of nasty names. I was shocked!

He ran upstairs in a terrible state.

I was taken aback. Then, when I thought he might have calmed down, I went upstairs, where I found him sobbing on his bed.

I put my arms around him and then started to explain things to him. I said that I thought he was old enough to understand the reasons why I had to leave his dad.

I said that Alan wasn't interested in making love to me, and that I had tried to get him to get help, but he refused. I told him that it was making me ill and that I didn't want to be on drugs because of it. Brian had also suffered at the hands of his father and knew what a terrible temper he had.

I promised him that I would do my best to get a job and find us somewhere to live. He seemed to understand and calmed down, and he never turned on me again. I have always tried to be honest with my children. I'm sure they respect you more.

After that, they went to stay with my mum and dad.

As I was only getting family allowance I started looking for a job. The local paper advertised one at a nearby public house as a waitress. I was so inexperienced and nervous that I kept dropping food on the floor. Many of the customers were businessmen, and they would deliberately drop items, so that they could see me bend down in my miniskirt. When I collected the plates, I had a job balancing them on my arms. Then I had to venture into the kitchen, where the two chefs were throwing knives at each other! One was Spanish and the other Irish.

The fat greasy Spaniard offered me money if I would sleep with him. Disgusted, I left without getting any money.

I went to see a doctor for more medication, even though it made me very sleepy. I also asked if I could go on the 'pill' (just in case).

I then bought *The Lady* magazine and saw an advertisement for a person to do artwork for a car salesman. There was also live-in accommodation, so I made an appointment to see him. The problem was, this was in Godmanchester, but nothing ventured nothing gained. So I got a Green Line bus, and after a long journey arrived at the pub where I had been told to get off at. I looked around at the empty car park, when suddenly an open-top sports car appeared. The driver was a middle-aged man whose face was covered with a bright red birthmark. He wore a large brimmed trilby hat that cast a shadow, and was obviously meant to hide his features. He asked my name, then opened the door and invited me to take a seat. We drove to a secluded bungalow set deep into the woods, and at that point I started to get scared. However, he was very nice and I went with him into his home.

He had a very nice bungalow, and after showing me around he then talked about his business. He produced the flyers that went onto the windows of new cars and needed someone to do the lettering. It seemed very easy to do, but boring.

He said that the place wasn't suitable for children, so we decided that the job wasn't for me. However, he drove me into town, and bought me a meal in a café. Then I got a train back to Hemel Hempstead. Looking back, I had taken a terrible risk, as nobody knew where I was.

At about this time we all went out for a meal. It must have been for a special occasion, as there were Doris and Fred, their son, who came up from London, their daughter and her husband, my mum and dad, Brian and Kevin and myself.

Doris's son had very strange eyes, and I was conscious of his gaze all through the evening.

After the meal, Mum and Dad took the boys back to theirs, and we went back to Crabtree Close.

Doris and Fred went up to bed, and their son and I were left sitting on the sofa. I cannot even remember his name and I didn't really like him; however, we started talking and he opened a bottle of wine (or maybe it was whisky). He kept asking me questions and pouring out more drink. I was so naive and a bit drunk, and I didn't realise I had fallen into his trap, and soon he was taking advantage of me. He was very experienced and we had sex for a long time, and in many positions.

Eventually we went upstairs, but he wanted to sleep alone in the spare double bed, so I had to retire to my little room alone. Doris always slept with her door wide open, and she had a mirror positioned so that she could see my door from her bed.

I don't recall much about the next day, except that Fred cleared up the front room and wouldn't look me in the eye. There was no sign of his son; he had gone back to London.

Sometime after that I was very ill. I woke up one morning bathed in perspiration, the sheets were soaked and I had a raging thirst. I must have dozed off again as it was late afternoon. I felt very weak and knew I needed a doctor. I tried calling out but there was no answer. Sometimes they, Doris and Fred, were out in the garden, or they might be out in the car. Somehow I managed to get down the stairs and to the phone in the hall. I found the doctor's number and asked for help. Shortly after I'd struggled back upstairs, someone rang the doorbell. I heard voices, then a doctor was shown into my room. He was appalled at the state I was in and immediately got Doris to get me some water. He said I shouldn't be living in such conditions. It was hot and there was no air in this tiny room. Doris returned with the water and said that she didn't even know I was in.

I cannot remember how long it took, but slowly I improved. I don't even know what was wrong with me. Doris hardly spoke to me after that, so I would sit in her other room by myself.

I decided to go to Tring and pay a visit to Ronnie and Penny. I told them what had happened to me, and Ronnie said I must get away as soon as possible. He also said that when I got somewhere to live, I would need an oven, and as he went to auctions he would look out for one for me.

After leaving theirs, I walked up the High Street and went to look in the do-it-yourself store. A very small drop-leaf table in the window caught my eye. It had a Formica top and was very cheap. I could do with this and it would go with the two stools that Mum was giving me.

The shop owner was a nice-looking man who was divorced, and he obviously knew who I was. He said he would keep the table for me. He asked for my address and suggested perhaps we could go out. I gave him my address, then caught the bus back to Hemel.

Some days later, I received a letter from him asking if he could pick me up and perhaps go to the pictures. He had signed it 'Clint', which of course wasn't his real name. I replied, and agreed a time and he came to collect me. I had asked him to stay in the car as I didn't want Doris to know my business. We didn't go to the pictures. He took me back to his shop, where he led me upstairs to his stockroom. To my surprise there was a mattress on the floor. He had it all worked out, so I went along with it.

It didn't last long and I was not impressed, but what really turned me off was the fact that he wore a wig! It was getting late by the time he dropped me off at Doris's. As I hadn't been given a key, I had to knock to be let in. She slept in the front and I knew she would hear me, but nobody opened the door. I had no money on me, so I couldn't get a bus or taxi, and even though it was bitterly cold, and they lived quite a long way away, I started to walk to my mother's.

She was amazed to see me at such a late hour, with my hair damp and wet and tears running down my cheeks. I was also out of breath. When I told her what had happened, she agreed with me that Doris must have heard me knock. She was very angry, as she already knew how I had been treated when I was ill. So after getting me a cup of tea and warming me up, she said that I wasn't to go back there.

I stayed at Mum's but the depression got so bad that I found it hard to recall certain things. Mum and Dad went round to Crabtree Close and had words. Of course, Doris said that she hadn't heard me, but Mum didn't believe her. They collected our personal belongings, but I think that my furniture was still in their garage.

I would go into town with Mum and go shopping, but I found it very hard to keep awake and often propped myself up against the supermarket shelves. One time I nearly fell into a chest freezer. I kept questioning what I had done. I had taken the boys away from their father, and I had nothing to offer them.

Also, I was too ill to hold down a job.

Moving On

My mum tried to help me find accommodation, looking at adverts and going to the council, but with no luck. The council had a long waiting list. I was getting more and more depressed.

Then mum had a brainwave.

My cousin Sylvia and her husband David lived in King's Lynn, and David and his father ran their own business, Hudson & Herring, renovating properties. Perhaps they might know of somewhere that I could rent…

So I rang David and as luck would have it, they were doing up some flats off Loke Road. David said that if I could get a train to King's Lynn, he would meet me at the station and take me to meet the landlord.

I don't know how I did it, but I got on a train, though I don't remember the journey. David was waiting for me on the platform when the train pulled into King's Lynn Station. David and Sylvia lived on Loke Road, and I remembered him from previous visits to Lynn with my parents. Dad's sister, Simone, lived with Peter and their son Billy in Queen Elizabeth Avenue, and my other cousin, Hazel, lived in Vancouver Avenue with her husband David King, so I had several relatives here.

David Hudson took me to Landles Estate Agents, which was close to the station. In an upstairs office I was introduced to the landlord. David did all the talking and he said he would be my guarantor. We were handed the keys to a flat in Harewood Drive and David took me to look at the property. A Mr Hare had built Harewood Drive, Harewood Parade and Harecroft Gardens after the war. They were all flats leading off Loke Road. Mine was at the bottom of a cul-de-sac, and Number 14 was upstairs. David's parents lived opposite, in a ground-floor flat.

There were garages at the end of Harewood Drive, and the

one that was closest to me was used by David and his dad for storing equipment for their business.

The front door opened onto the stairs leading up to a small landing, which had three doors.

To the right were two fairly large bedrooms, overlooking front and back, and to the left a living room which led into a small kitchen. Off of this was a bathroom with a toilet and sink; above the bath was a gas boiler. In the kitchen was another door that housed a larder with wooden shelves. There was a back door in the kitchen, which led onto a small landing where coal was stored. From this, a wooden staircase led down to an untidy garden, which was full of rubbish from the previous tenant.

There was a linen line attached to a pulley so that your washing would be very high up. You could see a lot of these lines about in this area and they certainly got a good blow!

The entire flat badly needed decorating and the garden cleared up, but I could see it all had potential.

My spirits lifted for the first time for weeks. This could all be mine for £3.50 per week. Somehow I would manage to afford that.

We looked more closely at what needed to be done.

There was a little coal in the bunker on the landing, but as it was summer, I wouldn't need any yet.

The bathroom walls had odd pieces of wallpaper on them, but otherwise the sink, bath and toilet just needed a good clean.

The boiler worked, though it was a bit difficult to light.

The kitchen ceiling had paint flaking off of it and the walls were painted dark green; however, the back door had panes of glass in it, and there was a small window beside the kitchen sink, which helped to lighten the place up.

The larder had a very tiny frosted glass window behind the shelves, which badly needed a good scrub. The walls and ceiling could all do with being painted white.

The living room had a fair-sized window looking out onto the road and the garages (where David and his dad kept their wood and paint etc.). There was a decent-sized fireplace with mottled brown tile surround, an alcove on either side, and a cupboard with a shelf, which would look better with the door off. (A job for

David?) The walls and ceiling needed attention, as did the bedrooms. The hallway and stairs also needed a lick of paint and brightening up.

There was plenty to do, and I couldn't wait to get started. I knew that I was capable of making this place into a lovely home for me and the boys.

Next, David showed me where the schools were, and they were not very far away. I would have to get this organised later on. He showed me where they lived and where the local shops and the launderette, and fish and chip shop were. Then we went back, paid a deposit and signed an agreement, and the flat was mine.

Elated, I went back to Hemel Hempstead and told Mum and Dad all about it. They were of course pleased for me, but were a bit apprehensive and said they would be sorry to see us go.

Following the removal van, we drove up to Lynn, with me and the boys travelling in the back of Dad's car. We dropped Brian and Kevin off at David and Sylvia's, as I would be staying with them there for a few days, and Mum and Dad would go to Simone's. This was while they helped me to sort out and clean the flat, before returning the boys back to Hemel. They were due to go back to Berkhamsted Comprehensive until I got their new schools sorted out in Lynn.

I think Mum and Dad were a bit shocked at the state of the flat. Luckily, Dad had sorted me out some tools and paint brushes. They also gave me two old stools and two old chests of drawers, which needed painting. There was also a very old blanket box, which they were given when they got married. Soon my few pieces were in situ. I was to sleep on the black plastic bed settee for now. It wasn't very comfortable, but it would do until I could afford a bed. Ronnie had kept his word and got me a little Belling electric oven, with three top plates and a grill.

All too soon, they all drove away, leaving me alone to make the flat habitable. The first thing I did was to throw all the antidepressant tablets down the toilet. This was to be the start of my new life.

Conclusion

This was the first part of my life – my life before Lynn. Later on, there would be many twists and turns, heartaches and a near death experience. But most of all, I would discover the real me.

Sheila Cordwell

Lightning Source UK Ltd.
Milton Keynes UK
24 August 2010

158938UK00001B/7/P